Whatsoever You Do Will Prosper

A Guide for Miraculous Prayer

D.W.Williams II

authorHOUSE°

AuthorHouse™
1663 Liberty Drive
Bloomington, IN 47403
www.authorhouse.com
Phone: 1 (800) 839-8640

Published by AuthorHouse 12/08/2015

ISBN: 978-1-5049-6607-8 (sc)
ISBN: 978-1-5049-6606-1 (e)

Library of Congress Control Number: 2015920094

Miracle Publishing Company
P.O. Box 275
Odenton, Maryland 21113

Table of Contents

This book is dedicated to my wife, Wendy N.Williams, and my two beautiful daughters, Noelle and Phoebe Williams. Remember, if you pray you will never fail and whatsoever you do will prosper!

Foreword

"What the church needs today is not more machinery or better, not new organizations or more novel methods, but men whom the Holy Ghost can use-men of prayer, men might in prayer. The Holy Ghost does not flow through methods, but through men. He does not come on machinery, but on men. He does not anoint plans, but men-men of prayer." E.M. Bounds

I believe that the church in America today is so anemic because prayer is no longer a major priority of the church. The discipline of prayer is waning in the lives of God's people individually as well as corporately, and if the church is going to be the powerful institution the Lord has ordained her to be, the church has to regain its pursuit and passion for prayer.

Pastor Donald Williams is one of the Lord's generals that is being used to ignite a reformation of prayer in the church. I met pastor Donnie when he was preparing himself for ministry at a seminary close to the church that I serve as the senior pastor. One of the scheduled times for prayer at our church is Monday through Friday from 5a.m. to 7 a.m. Pastor Donnie would be in our midst pursuing the Lord in prayer. He would not allow the rigors of seminary to keep him from inoculating the discipline of prayer. Prayer was not optional him. It was mandatory! He was devoted to prayer. Friday night from 7pm to 9pm we gathered together for a time for intercessory prayer. Quarterly we would begin prayer on Friday at 5a.m. and we would end at 5 a.m. on Sunday. Pastor Donnie served as the prayer pastor for our church. His passion and enthusiasm for prayer was so evident because he just didn't talk about prayer, he prayed.

Bishop Michael O. Brokenborough, Sr. Pastor of Household of Faith Deliverance Worship Center, Ardmore, Pennsylvania

Introduction

This book is not about accessing and acquiring material prosperity and success, but this book is about the power in praying prayers of faith that will release occurrences of miracles in every area of your life. From this point forward, you must believe and declare upon your life that the Heavenly Father will cause everything in your life to prosper – your family, your business, your ministry, your children, and everything that pertains to you. God is interested in you manifesting holistic prosperity that includes emotional, spiritual, financial, mental, physical, and relational prosperity. Make an agreement with yourself at this very moment that you will not allow any person, any cause, or any attack to uproot you from being planted in the presence of God. By the time you finish reading the introduction to this book, your hunger to pray and be in the presence of God will heighten. Everything in your life depends on prayer, and your current situation and situations to come will not be resolved until you cry out to the Lord as David cried unto the Lord, and the Lord heard Him and answered Him. You will begin to pray for things you've overlooked in the past, and things you never even knew mattered. You will also remember to pray about things you may have prayed for in the past that you may have neglected or given up on. Remember, you are deeply rooted and connected to God in the garden, surrounded by rivers of living water.

Before I started teaching prayer at different churches, I was under the impression that there is a right way to pray and a wrong way according to what I thought. God's Word teaches us that the only wrong way to pray is to pray outside the will of God, with only our will, or to not pray at all! **God's Word says, *"Now this is the confidence that we have in Him, that if we ask anything according to His will, He hears us, and if we know that He hears us, whatever we ask, we know that we have the petitions that we have asked of Him."* (1 John 5.14-15)**

Immediately after I read this passage, the Lord spoke to me and said, *"There are different ways to pray, according to My Word, that will strike My heart."* After this encounter with God, the desire to spend my life getting to know God through prayer intensified. I became hungry and thirsty for more of God's presence through prayer, and what I will share about prayer will cause your leaves not to wither!

Whatsoever You Do Will Prosper is a phrase that can be either an easy or tough pill to swallow because many people have given up on believing in the power of prayer. They have quit praying for many reasons, and two main reasons are because:

1.) They do not believe God exists and,

2.) When they prayed once nothing happened so they stopped praying because they expected immediate results.

When I first read Psalm 1 the latter portion of the 3rd verse says, "Whose leaf will not wither, but whatsoever he does will prosper;" and unfortunately these words did not mean anything to me. I was 9-years-old when my mother made me recite Psalm 1 every morning. By default I memorized the entire first Psalm and before long it was so engrained in my memory that I did not even have to use the Bible to read it any longer. Five years later, at the age of 14, I did not think much about these words, but since the word of God is living and powerful, these words became engrossed and imbedded in my body, soul, and spirit. When I went away for college I totally quit reciting the first chapter in Psalm, and I did not start reciting it again until the age of 26 when I decided to fully commit my life to the Lord. I remember one day I opened the New Living Translation Bible my mother had bought me when I was 16, and I turned to Psalm 1 and read it once. I closed the Bible and I said it from memory as if I had never forgotten it. It was a miracle because I had been so far away from God yet His Word was still present in my spirit, soul, and body. I felt excited, and at that point I realized how powerful His Word is, and that if I am planted at the living waters of His presence, whatever I do will prosper and my leaves will not wither. From my perspective, this phrase, "Whatever I do will prosper" was like winning billions of dollars. I realized that I do not have anything to fear or worry about because as long as I am planted in His presence, the healing living waters of the Spirit of God will run through my bloodline and no evil will befall me. I will be victorious! Whatever I touch will prosper. Whatever I pray for will go directly to the throne of the Lord Jesus Christ and it will be answered because I am planted.

The living waters that I am describing are the living waters that flow from the sanctuary of God. May the waters of the Holy Spirit flow to you from the throne and sanctuary of God to bring prosperity to you. May the living waters flow to you and cause you to prosper in every endeavor of life. May every problem you are faced with be solved by the Word of the Spirit. May your leaves not wither and may you bring forth fruit in this season. If you pray you will never fail!

Have you ever been ostracized, excluded, mistreated, or abused to the extent that you felt worthless? Do you believe you have insecurity and self-esteem issues? Have you committed a sin, repented, but remain feeling bad about that sin? Do you have trouble completing assignments, projects, and tasks? Is a relationship you are involved in unfruitful and ungodly? Is your marriage suffering? Are you experiencing financial difficulties and feeling emotionally drained?

Everyone on this earth, no matter what his or her economic status, needs to be engrafted into Jesus Christ. The God of heaven and earth made Himself available to everyone by sending His Son Jesus Christ to sympathize with *all* of our weaknesses, and He was tempted in every area, just as we are tempted, yet no sin was found in Him. Not only can Jesus Christ relate to us, but He sent His Spirit to help us with every situation. By His Divine power He has given us all things that pertain to life and godliness.

The very purpose of this book is to stir the spirit of prayer inside of you. It is designed to catapult your prayer life into the next dimension. The intent of this book is to help you to confidently believe and know that God's Word will come alive in you when you pray. You will also be able to adopt different ways of maneuvering in the spirit realm through various dimensions of prayer.

There is one way to begin making an imprint in the earth for the Kingdom of God, and this is to make this declaration upon every aspect of your very being: WHATEVER I DO WILL PROSPER! Does God not honor His word? Does every word that comes out of His mouth not accomplish and prosper? If you decree a thing, it will be established for you, so light will shine on your ways (Job 22.28 NKJV). Whatever you do will prosper, but it becomes even more powerful when you make God's Word personal to your life. Experience God's Word transform your reality. Every time you finish reading a few pages in this book, you will not be able to deny this direct truth that: WHATEVER YOU DO, from this point forward, WILL PROSPER!

50 Reasons Why Everything Depends on Prayer

1.) It is the only way to exercise higher level faith.

2.) Without prayer sin will prevail in one's life

3.) If we do not pray we cannot "be in the know" of God's plan

4.) Without prayer nations cannot be transformed

5.) Without prayer nations and people will not be healed of their diseases and sicknesses

6.) It's the open door to signs, wonders, and miracles

7.) It's the only way to understand the heart of God

8.) Without prayer transformation will not happen

9.) Without prayer mountains will not be moved

10.) If we don't pray there will be no guidance

11.) If we don't pray vision will not be developed

12.) Without praying God will not know your voice

13.) If we don't pray we will not know God's voice

14.) Without prayer ministries and churches cannot truly flourish

15.) Without prayer we cannot glorify God

16.) Without prayer the prophetic word cannot go forth

17.) Without prayer God will not release His glory

18.) Without prayer we will not have joy

19.) Without prayer we cannot experience peace

20.) Without prayer we cannot have patience

21.) Without prayer we cannot know God

22.) Without prayer we cannot endure temptations

23.) Without prayer we will not have wisdom

24.) Without prayer we cannot make godly decisions

25.) Without prayer we can't defeat Satan and his angels

26.) Without prayer we cannot please God

27.) Without prayer corrupt leaders will not become incorrupt

28.) Without prayer we will not have power

29.) Without prayer we cannot represent God

30.) Without prayer we cannot perform the works of Christ

31.) Without prayer people cannot be saved

32.) Without prayer hearts will not be softened

33.) Without prayer repentance will not take place

34.) Without prayer revival will not happen in different regions

35.) Without prayer the baptism of the Holy Spirit will not happen

36.) Without prayer demons will not flee

37.) Without prayer chains will not break

38.) Without prayer sensitivity to the Holy Spirit will not be sensed

39.) Without prayer your anointing will not be potent

40.) Without prayer marriages will fail

41.) Without prayer finances will plummet

42.) Without prayer there will be no movement in people's lives

43.) Without prayer failure will often occur

44.) Without prayer we cannot receive necessary and true promotions of ordination

45.) Without prayer strongholds cannot be brought down

46.) Without prayer missions cannot be accomplished

47.) Without prayer we cannot endure hardships, persecution, and trials

48.) Without prayer we will not possess a willingness to suffer

49.) Without prayer problems cannot be solved

50.) Without prayer there will be no release of revelation.

CHAPTER I

Nothing Happens Until You Pray!

I t wasn't until Solomon prayed a simple prayer that he truly experienced the overwhelming love and favor God wanted him to experience. In fact, the favor and blessings Solomon received were not achieved because of Solomon's intelligence, networks, and luck. What he received was given to him by God and God alone. What I admire about Solomon is that he understood what he was getting into as it related to his kingship. However, Solomon had to endeavor in self-examination in order for him to realize that he lacked what he needed in order to be a successful king. Solomon knew his shortcomings and his weaknesses. The Bible says that Solomon burned one thousand incense sticks as a sacrificial offering to the Lord and the Lord appeared to him and said,

"What do you want? Ask, and I will give it to you!" (1 Kings 3.5cNKJV)

If you want to get the attention of God then worship Him. This isn't a formula to get what you want from the Lord, but when you truly worship the Father, He sees your heart and examines it, and then He determines what you can handle. Offering worship to the Lord triggers God to inherently give us His heart, and when we have His heart we possess His desires for our lives. This explains why when we pray God will grant us the desires of our heart. The Bible says, *"Delight yourself also in the Lord, and He will give you the desires of your heart."* (Psalms 37.4NKJV) When we delight ourselves in the Lord, we are actually delighting ourselves into the things that make God joyful. The delights of God become our delight, which causes our desires to be in agreement with what is in God's heart. Walking in agreement with God advances our prayers that cause God to grant us what is in our heart.

Solomon was able to pray a simple prayer when he could have prayed for donors, investors, generals and captains, land, highly intelligent political councils, and so much more. In verse 9 Solomon asks, *"God give me a heart of understanding...that I may discern from good and evil."* (1 Kings 3.9)

This prayer is powerful because Solomon does not ask for material things, but his request strikes God's heart for Him to initiate something that can only be birthed inside of Solomon; and that is integrity! The Bible says, "the speech pleased the Lord, that Solomon had asked this thing" (1 Kings 3.10 NKJV). Solomon prays for a heart of understanding that will cause his decision making to be grounded, rooted, and saturated with a spirit of godly integrity. As a result, God not only granted Solomon's request for wisdom and an understanding heart, but also riches and fame; and He said no other king would be compared to Solomon for the rest of his life. Your prayer life is about to be turned so upside down and inside out that the miracles the Lord will unleash in your life and all around you will be miracles you have never experienced. Just as there has never been a king like Solomon, the miracles you are going to experience will be meticulously patterned and designed for you. Your life will never be the same!

It's amazing because God has given us everything we need according to life and godliness and we have had this power since our very first day of life. But His word tells us we should seek Him and His righteousness and everything else will be added to us. There are a few things you must know about the power God has given you, and one of the first things you must realize and accept is that you do not lack anything. You have everything you need according to life and godliness, but God wants to give you more so that you may reflect His glory. I believe the Lord wants us to (re) present Him to the world with integrity. God is willing to do anything to cause us to (re)present Him with excellence to the world. Therefore, God wants to enhance what He has given you so that people who are observing and evaluating your life will grow in greater trust and faith in Christ Jesus.

God had already given Solomon His heart because Solomon prayed for something that was already in God's plans for him. Because Solomon knew exactly what God wanted for Him, God added to Solomon's life. You lack nothing. You are very capable of reflecting the image of God, but God wants to make additions. When God added to Solomon's life things started happening for him, and there was movement. God made Solomon's name great throughout the earth and people from other parts of the world found out who he was. People travelled from near and far to meet him. Because of one simple prayer that came from a heart of worship, Solomon received so much favor that he went in to owning and governing countries, cities, villages, highways, rivers, businesses of raw materials, and many modes of transportation.

Worship leads us to prayer, and it is an act of intimacy and adoration that literally causes us to ignite the heart of God. God's heart catches on fire when we worship Him, and when we worship in Spirit and in truth we are consumed with the Holy fire of God. We literally strike God's heart when we worship Him in Spirit and in Truth. This is the level of worship He is seeking, and God is still seeking nations of people that will worship Him not only in the setting of worship gatherings, but in the privacy of their prayer space.

Before you request anything of God you must first relinquish what you want for those moments and give yourself away unto the Lord. The attitude of worship should always be consumed in us giving to God. I understand why Jesus says He is seeking a generation of worshipers that will worship Him in "spirit" because if we worship God from the flesh our worship will never be His will, but what our mind believes we need and want from God. That type of worship is selfish rather than selflessness honor to the Lord. Solomon knew what pleased God when it came to engaging in intimacy with God because he learned worship from his father, King David. He knew that sacrifice, a denial and rejection of what he wanted, was necessary in order for Him to get things done on God's terms. In order for whatever you do to prosper, you must come to Christ Jesus and relinquish the demands you place on God.

I remember when the Lord led me to organize a prayer shut-in and one of the first portions of the prayer night began with three hours of worship. We were shut-in for 72 hours and there were so many things the Lord wanted us to pray for. The instructions the Lord first gave me was for us to spend three hours on a prayer target. However, before we asked God for anything, the first three hours were spent adoring the Lord and reverencing His presence. Aside from the prayer shut-in, I often notice how hard it is for some people to spend time worshiping for one hour. One of the reasons why some people are challenged and distracted during a set worship time is because some people are concerned with their time and what they have to do in the coming hours of the day. Can you imagine how God feels when we spend most of our time in His presence asking rather than basking? We must not be concerned about the future events of our agendas, but we must be concerned with what God desires for us during the 'now' while worshiping Him.

Solomon offered one thousand burning incense sticks unto the Lord because he wanted to release a sweet aroma unto the Lord. He ultimately wanted God to be pleased with his worship. Can you imagine how long that must have taken him? It's amazing how Solomon worshiped God with such intensity. When we recognize that we truly need God to intervene in our lives we must be determined to relentlessly give God an unyielding giving away of ourselves and everything that pertains to us. God's plan for our lives are so great that we must realize that we cannot fulfill these plans on our own accord and on our terms, but they must be performed by His Spirit! Solomon was a premeditated worshipper. Earlier that day Solomon decided to lay it all out before the Lord. He planned to climb and hike Mt. Gibeah, get to the highest point to draw nearer to God, and then offer one thousand burnt incense sticks to the Most High. Solomon went through desperate measures to be with God. Plan to be with God today, tomorrow, and forever. Plan to spend your day with the Lord. Develop a hunger and thirst for worship and be willing to do whatever it takes to be in the presence of the Lord.

God loves when His people are willing to go through desperate measures just to get to His heart. He loves it when our attitudes communicate, *"No matter what I have to go through, I'm going to draw closer to Him because He has what I need."* That was the attitude of the woman who bled for years upon years. She fought through the crowd while getting pushed, pulled, caught, and shoved. I'm certain she even had to crawl a few times to get to Jesus. The crowd that surrounded Jesus probably perceived this woman to be insane, but she fought her way through because she was at a point of desperation. She refused to bleed for another day. She refused to live with the foul odor of blood. She refused to go through clothing after clothing because she bled uncontrollably. She refused to be bed-ridden. She mustered up the energy to reach Jesus because she wanted to be healed. What are you willing to do to get to the heart of God? What are you willing to throw away in order to reach His heart? How many incense sticks are you willing to burn to get the attention of God? What are you going to burn? What are you going to allow God to burn inside of you?

Are you worried about things not going as you expect? Are you experiencing problems, which are causing you to be stressed? Do you need to be refreshed with a renewed sense of self? Do you need newness in your life that seems like it's not happening?

Nothing happens until a prayer is prayed. There is no movement, no enhancement, no expansion, no progress, no profit, no productivity, no protection, no promotion, no clarity, no understanding, no release, no freedom, and no burden lifted until a prayer is prayed. Demons do not move until a prayer is prayed. If you find yourself in a financial cycle of mistakes, then pray! There can be no financial breakthrough until there is a change in spending behavior and dedication of the finances to the Lord through prayer. There is no favor, no blessing, and no miracle until a prayer is prayed. There is no purpose, no meaning, no significance, and no true sense of living found until a prayer is prayed. Nothing can be done until a prayer unto the Almighty God is prayed.

Satan's plan of deception is to cause you to believe that with everything that is taking place in your life, whether positive or negative, you can go days upon days without seeking the face of the Lord. A common mistake many believers make is experiencing victories and losses and believing they can go days, weeks, months, or even years while neglecting to seek the face of God. Victories should cause us to pray more, and losses should cause us to pray with even greater intensity.

I knew of a person who experienced great torment in the area of employment and a relationship with someone he courted. Things seemed to be going terribly for him. The courting dynamics were not biblically grounded, his financial slump seemed to be weighing in on him, and his employment situation was not aligned with his passions.

Every morning he woke up with anger in his heart and he was very frustrated with life, but he ultimately wanted to experience a change in his life. Something motivated him to call me for advice. He told me what he was experiencing and the first thing I asked him was if he had prayed about his situation. He told me he did not think this was a matter of prayer. Even though he had been plagued with depression and frustration for about five months, he told me that he did not think his problem was big enough to bring to the Lord's attention.

You must understand that failing to pray will result in human rationalization that can cause major stagnation, especially when it comes to God's will being fulfilled in your situation. Some people look to all sorts of coping mechanisms rather than entering into the presence of God's rest. There is nothing too hard for God. There is no problem too big for God to handle, and no sickness too terminal for God to heal. There have been times when I needed God to move in His power in my life, and I remember praying to Him because I knew He would intervene; but after a while I would suddenly stop praying about that particular issue because I grew impatient. Over time, I noticed there was still no change, no resolve, and no renewal. It was at that point that I realized I was not truly committed to praying for God's answer to that particular problem. **Do you know that when we stop praying, we stop believing?** An abrupt ceasing to pray will cause someone to look for answers outside of God's wisdom and knowledge. God's wisdom is infinite and His ways are not our ways; but His ways are pure and will cause us to prosper. Every good and perfect gift comes from God and He adds no sorrow with the gifts He gives.

Expect a visitation from an angel of the Lord. Expect a word of instruction from the Holy Spirit. Expect Him to give you even more than what you ask for. Expect God to move on your behalf. When you worship the Most High God, and you submit your heart to the Lord, know that your prayers will no longer be your prayers; your prayers will be His desires for you. And your leaf will not wither, and whatsoever you do will prosper. God will add more of what you need to guarantee your prosperity. Let the King of Glory come in and invade your strategy so that you may see how His strategy will bring you into a place of prosperity and victory. Without prayer, nothing happens…

CHAPTER II

The Power of Repentance

"Without repentance, there is no freedom, no breakthrough, and no escape; you will remain imprisoned. Get out of prison!"

Twelve reasons why repentance is powerful:

1.) Repentance will cause us to understand the depth, height, length, and width of God's everlasting, unchanging, and unfailing love

2.) New things occupies and replaces the space where the old formerly occupied

3.) Repentance always reconciles us to God

4.) Repentance supernaturally makes us vulnerable to receive and accept God's plan and purpose for our lives

5.) Repentance causes the healing of sicknesses, diseases, and nations

6.) Repentance releases God's favor upon us rather than wrath, which is the consequence of rebelling against God

7.) Repentance enables us to crave for truth

8.) Repentance strengthens faith in Christ Jesus

9.) Repentance causes deliverance and destroys demonic activity

10.) Repentance converts non-believers into believers of Christ Jesus

11.) Repentance rejects anything that is counterfeit

12.) Repentance leads to rejecting traditions of men.

The enemy has deceived the church into believing that repentance will not bring about a renewal and reconciliation with God. There are many reasons why people do not repent and turn from their sins, but one reason is a lack of faith in Christ Jesus that they will be totally free. **Repentance is the gateway to freedom.** The Holy Spirit has allowed His true prophets to hear the heart of God that is crying out for His people to repent from their sins, traditions, habits, and openness to messages that do not bring His people back to Him. What is most disheartening about the church's current condition is that many leaders of God's people are operating under the satanic anointing of Eli. During Eli's occupation of holding the office of the high priest, God sent two prophets to warn Eli that destruction was coming if he did not discontinue his wickedness and discipline his sons for their wickedness. Eli responded to the prophet Samuel with a spirit of indifference when Samuel warned and rebuked Eli by saying, "It is the Lord, let Him do what seems good to Him." (1 Sam. 3.18) I do not interpret Eli's response to Samuel as an exaltation and glorification of God, but I believe Eli is saying that at this point in his life, he is not willing to make a change and there is nothing he can do; so let God be God and do what He is going to do anyway.

Eli possessed this attitude of pride and lethargy, and the opportunity of repenting from greed and abusing the offerings of sacrifice would not free him from the snare of the enemy. Even when Eli attempted to discipline his sons, his sons disobeyed him because Eli disobeyed God; and Eli made no plans to consider repentance as an option. Eli was a corrupt priest and his sons participated in the corruption despite the fact that they were of the highest order of priesthood. Because Eli had no control, no backbone, and no authority to discipline his sons, God held Eli and his sons accountable for their sin. The problem with Eli, like the church, is two-fold:

1.) Eli lost hope in repentance, which lends the loss of hope in God, and

2.) Dangerously being complacent with disobedience.

The mindset Eli possessed is one in the same with the mindset some believers have towards prayers of repentance. They have lost hope in repentance and they have become numb to the chastisement of God. **The reason why rejecting God's chastisement is dangerous is because our rejection of God's chastisement communicates to God that His love is not worth what He has done at the cross!**

Deception

Deception is dangerous and detrimental because it is hard for many people to identify when they are being deceived. I've noticed people not wanting to confess and admit that something or someone has deceived them. **Deception causes many problems but two main problems it causes, is for people to live in denial, and for them to be the victim of abuse. In fact, deception *is* abuse.** Deception is not concerned with prayer, family, marriage, love, justice, wisdom, knowledge, your salvation in Christ Jesus, your finances, your health, your sanity, your well-being, your livelihood, your pancreas, your lungs, your heart, your future, or anything else. Rather, deception is concerned with causing people to fail, be depressed, be tormented, lose sleep, live in greed, remain prideful, be sick, have a broken spirit, experience stagnation, search for love in all of the wrong places, cause insecurity, and much more. Anything that causes any of these issues must be dealt with by repenting from a mindset that you refuse to reject. *Metanoia* is the Greek translation of the word 'Repentance,' and it means to have a change of heart and mind about a matter of sin, shortcomings, and/or faults. When deception arises and you attempt to petition God for blessing and favor, God, because of His grace and mercy, may grant your prayer requests, but He is not necessarily obligated to answer the prayer. I believe God is more reluctant to answering prayers for material blessings rather than His eagerness to answer prayers of repentance.

Because of rebellious attitudes and behavior toward God many people that may receive grandiose favor could possibly be deceivingly blessed. Deception is so abusive that the enemy will cause believers to believe that God is the source of some answered prayers and blessings. Just as God allowed the adversary, Satan, in the Book of Job to have control over destroying Job's life, God can give the adversary permission to bless. Recall in 1 Kings 22 when king Jehoshaphat and Ahab sought 400 prophets to ask them if they should go to war against Ramoth-gilead and the 400 prophets said, "Yes, go right ahead! The Lord will give the king victory" (1 Kings 22.6 NLT). Then they wanted a confirmation and decided to ask the prophet Micaiah who never prophesied anything anyone ever wanted to hear and he prophesied to them saying, "In a vision I saw all Israel scattered on the mountains, like sheep without a shepherd. And the Lord said, 'There master has been kill. Send them home in peace'" (1 Kings 22.17 NLT). The kings knew that what Micaiah told them was not the truth so they begged him to tell them what God says. Subsequently, Micaiah gave more insight to his prophesy to the kings and said,"

> *"Listen to what the Lord says! I saw the Lord sitting on His throne with all the armies of heaven around Him, on his right and on his left. And the Lord said, 'Who can entice Ahab to go into battle against Ramoth-gilead so he can be killed?' "There were many suggestions, and finally a spirit approached the Lord and said, 'I can do it!' "'How will you do this?' the Lord asked. "And the spirit replied, 'I will go out and inspire all of Ahab's prophets to speak lies.' "'You will succeed,' said the Lord. 'Go ahead and do it.' "So you see the Lord has put a lying spirit in the mouths of all your prophets. For the Lord has pronounced your doom."* (1 Kings 22.19-23 NLT)

King Jehoshaphat and king Ahab were not only deceived by their army strength, artillery, power, and hierarchical prominence, but they were also deceived by prophets that prophet-lied about their destiny. Many are deceived by some scientific and biological theories, fortune cookies, horoscope insights, social media personality and aura tests, prominence, power, education achievements, and hierarchical positions. These phenomena can cause people to lose trust, reliance, and confidence in God and prayer. Deception is dangerous; stay away from it. If you do not know if you are deceived about anything in your life ask God to reveal all areas where you could be deceived and he will answer your prayer. Once God reveals these areas to you, confess your sins and truly repent from ungodly mindsets. The outcome of deception will cause you to rely on your own strengths and abilities rather than possessing a perpetual reliance on the Holy Spirit. If you do not rely on the Holy Spirit, you will find yourself in a state of a spiritual drought and famine. The river will become dry and the living waters will not feed the tree that is planted by the rivers of God.

I met a young couple that told me they wanted Christ to be at the center of their relationship, and they decided to get married at the local courthouse. Their finances failed them, they were always at each other's throats, and the young lady's husband eventually abandoned her. As I counseled them before they got married, I suggested that they continue receiving godly counsel by a pastor and eventually wait sometime before they would get married. They neglected to faithfully attend Bible study, receive pastoral counseling, and prayer; and because they neglected to put Christ at the center of everything, everything fell apart for them.

The message I have for the church is to accept the voice of correction and rebuke for the lack of discernment of allowing secularism to infiltrate the doctrines of ministries and churches. Don't muzzle the ox and don't behead the prophet of this hour. Do not be deceived! Harden not your heart as during the day of rebellion. Repentance will bring about newness in the lives of God's people that will resemble moves of God and revivals noted in Scripture. Pray to the Lord for prophets of God to speak to the body with a boldness to proclaim times of refreshing.

Pray that the Lord will send someone into your life that will share God's plans for your life. Pray that you find someone who will speak with you using the wisdom of God. Maybe before you pray, open your Bible and read Proverbs and know that wisdom is crying out in the market place, but only a few can hear its sound. Ask God to open your ears to the sound of godly wisdom, and make your ears deaf to the sound of folly.

Self-condemnation and deception collectively work together in order to destroy the vigor you need to pray. After Adam and Eve partook of the fruit, the Bible says,

> *"The eyes of both of them were opened and they knew that they were naked; and they sewed fig leaves together and made themselves coverings. And they heard the sound of the Lord God walking in the garden in the cool of the day, and Adam and his wife hid themselves from the presence of the Lord God among the trees of the garden."* (Genesis 3.7,8 NKJV).

Adam and Eve knew they were disobedient to God. When the Bible says "their eyes were opened" it suggests they *realized* and received the ability to see things which they previously never realized and understood. In their case, they were privy to the reality of their sin that caused them to lose their freedom of being naked. The loss of this freedom led them to cover up their sin with guilt and so they condemned themselves. They were convicted because they knew they were not free in the liberty they once had. This self-condemnation led them to deceive themselves into thinking they can hide from God. Because of God's mercy and grace God preserved their ability to hear His voice and to discern His presence. God could have easily stripped Adam and Eve of the privilege to hear His voice and discern His presence. Please believe that

> *"...God who is rich in mercy, because of His great love with which He loved us, even when we were dead in trespasses, made us alive together with Christ, and raised us up together, and made us sit together in heavenly places in Christ Jesus, that in ages to come He might show the exceeding riches of His grace in His kindness toward us in Christ Jesus."* (Eph. 2.4)

In light of prayer, condemnation and deception will cause us to judge ourselves and believe the anti-Christ ideology, which teaches that God does not want us in His presence. Just like Adam and Eve, we cover ourselves based on human understanding, and the truth is that the only covering that preserves us is the blood of Jesus. Not only do people try to cover their sins, but some people attempt to hide from God. This happens because they believe they can justify their sins, but we have been justified by faith through Christ Jesus (Romans 5.1 NKJV). We cannot cover our sins from Christ and be reconciled with peace to Christ Jesus, and that is, oftentimes, the mindset of some believers. This is a deception believers adopt into their understanding about sin. The enemy loves when believers get to this level of believing their own deceptive thoughts about how "God works." This is not how the Lord works! Remember God's first question to Adam? "Where are you?" Most of the time, we are asking, "Where is God?" But God is saying, "Where are you?"

It is not in the nature of God's character to leave us in sin and away from Him, but it is in God's nature for Him to look for us. **God loved Adam and Eve so much that He chased after them when they hid from Him.**

It is one thing to discuss how sin hinders prayers, but self-condemnation and deception are just as detrimental to our relationship with God as any other sin. Condemnation inhibits us from living out our authority and power that was given to us from Christ Jesus. It is only through prayer that we can accept and utilize power and authority, and if condemnation and deception hinders us from coming into the presence of God, then we will never be able to utilize our authority and power. Without prayer, we cannot fight in the war against demon spirits, powers, principalities, and spiritual wickedness in heavenly places. Not only does condemnation inhibit us from using our divine authority and power, but it keeps us from praying to the Lord and entering into His presence.

Although the enemy has deceived people in many areas, such as prayer and repentance, deception spreads in people's thoughts. Whenever someone declares the truths found in the Scriptures and expounds upon them with integrity, the enemy likes to put thoughts into the minds of God's people about the truth. The enemy shrewdly and cleverly influences people to own those thoughts and make them a part of their attitude.

I have experienced this happen with people so many times, especially when I minister about friendships and relationships. I often suggest to certain people to choose individuals as friends that have their ear connected to the heart of God. God's people should receive insight and advice from friends that are in tune with God's word and what the Holy Spirit is saying. The Bible says in Jer. 23.18, *"For who has stood in the counsel of the Lord, and has perceived and heard His word? Who has marked His word and heard it?"* No one has to claim to be a prophet to say what they believe God wants for His people, but you must be careful when receiving advice from individuals who say they have your best interest at heart that truly does not have your best interest in mind. When I share this Biblical perspective with individuals that do not see anything wrong with their friendships and the advice of their friends that leads them to ungodliness, one of the most popular arguments I hear is, "Why do I have to give up those friendships and cut them off?" Well, when you consider the promises of God, His plans for your life, and how valuable His plans are for your life, you must observe those relationships you are involved in to be confident in knowing that they agree with what God wants for you. We should be willing to receive council and advice from individuals that see things from God's perspective and not based on humanism. There is a way that seems right unto man, but the end thereof leads to destruction. No one can ever go wrong with offering prayer as a solution for receiving guidance from God about a particular circumstance. The reality is that so many people can influence our lives and situations but that does not mean that any of the variety of solutions is God's solution for our lives. God wants us to prosper in every way possible and He has written the following in His word:

> *"The righteous should choose their friends carefully, for the way of the wicked leads them astray."* (Proverbs 12. 26)

He also spoke in His word to:

> *"Do not be deceived: Evil company corrupts good habits."* (1 Cor. 15.33 NKJV)

The problem with deception in these cases is that deep down, those who are living in deception have a gut feeling that what God's Word says is true and correct, but the enemy comes along and whispers lies into the minds of God's people. The enemy will make an argument for his claim just as he did with Eve. And this is how the enemy persuades us to believe that his lies are our genuine sentiments.

What I am communicating in this chapter is similar to what the enemy has achieved with many churches as it relates to cessation, the offices of apostles and prophets, healing and deliverance, marriage, divorce, gambling, fleshly vices, and many other areas. To paraphrase the serpent's words to Eve, the serpent asked Eve to, *"Consider what is around you, how could what God says be true?"* What God has established in His word and what He has spoken is truth!

Eli's mind was warped with deception and because he was deceived by his own ways, his sons could never accept correction and rebuke. The same idea goes for the church. God is calling us to repentance and He is attempting to get the attention of the leaders first. If God can chastise the leaders and the leaders accept the word of correction and rebuke, the church will respond in repentance. Because Eli refused to repent, God removed His glory from Israel. The spirit of Ichobod embodied Israel and it took years for God to restore His glory to Israel. In fact, the next time we are taught about God's restored glory was when Solomon finished the temple and the worship was pleasing to the Lord. The Bible says, *"The Temple was filled with the glory of God!"* The Lord wants to fill the earth with knowledge in Christ Jesus as the waters cover the sea. This knowledge cannot be ascertained until there is a breaking of the heart of stone and the reception of a heart of flesh. God wants to get through to you just as He repeatedly attempted to get through to Eli. How long does the Lord have to warn us by what He allows to happen in this world before we cast down our idols? What more does the Lord have to do in order for us to respond with, "I repent!" God sent plague, disaster, and pestilence upon pestilence to Egypt in order for Pharaoh to finally believe that there is nobody like the Almighty God.

My daily prayer is that we would change our mind, attitude, and perspective about issues of the world that we have allowed to become doctrine taught in churches. These worldly doctrines of demons are being taught and accepted by a non-discerned people. Our hearts have been hardened to repentance, and in order for us to truly prosper we must have a heart of repentance toward the things He is concerned with transforming. If we do not accept repentance we will miss out on experiencing refreshing times; and refreshing times are upon us! Repent, and your leaves will not wither, but whatsoever you do will prosper!

CHAPTER III

Praying in the Power of the Holy Spirit

"Praying always with all prayer and supplication in the Spirit, being watchful to this end with all perseverance and supplication for all saints" (Ephesians 6.18 NKJV)

Water is great to drink but if you mix fruit in water you would maximize the benefits of both the fruit and water. Although fruits have their advantages, lemons are one of the most powerful fruits to use for everything in life. If you were to cut a lemon into three slices, separate the flesh from the peel, and put the flesh into a bottle of water, your body will become stronger. Some of the benefits of lemons are as follows:

Lemons provide electrolytes to hydrate the body;

Lemons give you calcium and magnesium;

Lemons reduce the pain in the joints;

Lemons cause the liver to produce more enzymes than any other food;

Lemons release toxins, purify the liver; prevent cancer and gingivitis;

Lemons suppress hunger cravings and help with weight loss;

Lemons help to dissolve gall, pancreatic, and kidney stones and calcium deposits;

Lemons relieve heartburn… And so much more!

I drink between 60-80 ounces of lemon water a day and my health has tremendously changed as a result. Although I did not write this chapter to discuss lemons, I found that like drinking lemon water as a lifestyle, praying in the power of the Spirit will cause your prayers to unleash power in miraculous ways. It is one thing to drink water, but it is another thing to drink lemon water. Likewise, it is great to pray, but it is even greater to pray in the power of the Holy Spirit.

In January 2010, my wife and I lived in the house of one of our close sisters in Christ. During the month of January we went on a church fast for 21 days. As we were fasting, Aunt Courtney, the owner of the house we stayed in, encouraged me to pray in the power of the Holy Spirit day and night. After I learned that she habitually prayed in the power of the Spirit, I was impressed and became more committed to praying in the Spirit myself. Aunt Courtney was more than a sister in Christ. She was more a mother in Christ; a general in God's Kingdom. Although praying in the Spirit is filled with so much power, one of the outcomes of praying in the Spirit is when you pray in this manner you approach the spirit realm head on without any fear while bringing down the kingdom of darkness. Before I learned that Aunt Courtney prayed in the power of the Spirit, I thought I was the only person in the world to spend hours praying in the Spirit. I was excited, relieved, and curious to hear the revelation God gave her concerning praying in the Spirit. Even after I learned that she prayed in the Spirit, everything I originally discerned about her added up correctly: she walked in power, authority, faithfulness, holiness, and love. My Jesus, she was an example that I needed to meet in order for my prayer life to go onto a greater dimension. Although I was committed to praying in the Spirit, Aunt Courtney gave me more confidence that praying in the Spirit was not strange, but what the Lord desires.

Do you realize that because Adam and Eve disobeyed God's instructions our communication with God became flawed? Do you also realize that because of Jesus' eternal act of salvation our communication access to God was restored? It is interesting that Adam was able to name and rule the animals, and have dominion over creation, but after their disobedience, Adam and Eve could no longer live in that same full authority and power. When Jesus was led to fast and pray in the wilderness for forty days and nights, Satan attempted to stop Christ from bringing us into sonship. As Satan consistently attempted to tempt Jesus, Satan knew that if Jesus overcame temptations we would have power and authority to also overcome Satan and his plans. Praying in the Spirit is powerful because when we pray in the Spirit, our act of prayer reminds Satan that we have power and authority to overcome him and his plans. When we pray in the Spirit, we literally disrupt the planned attack of the enemy.

For thousands of years, humans have constructed and reconstructed, structured and restructured, modified and re-modified communication. To this day, humanity continues to struggle with communication. Communication is so flawed that humans were previously confident in each other's communication skills, whereas now, the human race's personal and interpersonal communication skills have drastically plummeted. This generation's idea of dating and meeting is achieved through virtual means. Men and women meet via social media outlets and dating online in order to live out their love affairs. Sometimes when I go to restaurants I see married couples and unmarried couples that are dating. And I notice that there is no in-depth conversation because their cell phones distract them. What is also interesting is that nowadays, people choose pictures of celebrity and animal faces called *memes* in order to share how they feel about something and these *memes* are used through text messaging. Not only that, but people can choose to ignore a text or call if they do not feel like speaking at any particular moment.

If you could understand how flawed our communication skills are, then you can imagine how damaged our communication skills are with the Lord. Our communication skills with the Lord can include praying, meditating, reciting His word, and thinking about God. **God has given us His written word to declare; yet declarations and mindsets are sometimes contrary to His written word!** Many times we rely on our inconsistent emotions to talk to a never-changing Savior. Therefore, when we pray prayers that are not aligned in the will of the Father it does not intimidate demons, sickness, finances, marriage, family, and government. It is normal to get emotional while praying but we should not pray prayers that are *out*side the will of the Lord. David cried out to the Lord and the Lord heard him, which lets us know that God heard him, but David's prayer was grounded in truth. When our emotions are going rampant we can rely on the Holy Spirit because when we do not know what to pray for, the Holy Spirit will intercede for us with groaning that cannot be uttered according to the will of God. Praying in the power of the Holy Spirit causes us to pray with a mindset of truth while our emotions may feel the total opposite of what we are praying.

Jesus Christ redeemed us from sin and as a result, our dominion and authority has been restored. Jesus disarmed principalities and powers, and He made a public spectacle of the devil by triumphing over them in it. Not only has the power in our word been restored, but it has become ignited with fire, whereby the Almighty God has given us a purified language. This purified language is meant for believers to accurately communicate with the Almighty King through praying in the power of the Spirit!

If you pray in the power of the Holy Spirit, you will experience the benefits of prayer when praying in the Spirit because this type of prayer is according to God's Word. The Bible states we should pray in the Spirit always (Ephesians 6.18a NKJV). I wish everyone would drink lemon water. In fact, I tell everyone I meet to drink lemon water. But I say to you, "Pray in the Spirit!" If you pray in the Spirit sometimes, begin praying in the Spirit always! If you have not been baptized with the Holy Spirit, ask the Lord to baptize you with His Holy Spirit. After you ask, move your lips and sound your voice and you will miraculously begin praying in the power of the Holy Spirit. Do not stop, but pray always in the Spirit! There is so much power involved with praying in the Spirit that I find this book a challenge to finish writing because I am motivated to stop and pray in the Spirit.

What I find to be extremely interesting about language is how flawed languages are. When we read the Bible, many theologians and Bible scholars try their best to translate words that derive from the ancient Hebrew, Aramaic, and Greek languages. Some scholars translated and transliterated God's Word by the guidance of the Holy Spirit, hoping to remain faithful to God's original meaning. Other scholars have stretched and abused the truth of God's Word by totally redefining salvation and replacing some words with other words. *Whatsoever You Do Will Prosper* is not about the original language of the Bible nor is it about how various Bible groups promote their human designed agenda into God's Word. This book is about living next to the waters of the Lord where His throne is exalted. This is about sitting before the King, the Fountain of Life that releases waters which are potent for our lives. He is the Living Water that causes your leaves not to wither, and whatsoever you do will prosper! The way you remain planted by the rivers of living water is to remain prayerful. When you pray, you are in His presence. No matter how distant you may believe you are, when you call on the name of Jesus, He immediately answers.

Some believers have lost faith in prayer and have quit praying because they prayed to God about problems, desires, expectations, and requests. Something has caused them to believe that God has not answered their prayers. Other believers have prayed to the Almighty God according to His will and experienced tremendous miracles because they prayed the will of the Father into their situation. I believe most believers in Christ Jesus pray in their native language without realizing nor acknowledging the flaws in their language. There are many necessary components to survival, but I believe there are two especially pertinent components to survival and they are water and communication.

In general, every language is a melting pot of universal words used to assist humans with communicating in a precise, concise, and accurate manner. Over time, words have become obsolete, deleted, changed, modified, and replaced with other words to more accurately communicate. **Language has evolved, and language will continue to evolve; but the heavenly language of the Almighty King is timeless**. Therefore, praying in the power of the Holy Spirit is the language of the Almighty Savior, and His language will never change. **Praying in the Spirit is using God's supernatural word to communicate to Him for whatever is in your heart.** Jesus said to His disciples, *"The words I speak are Spirit and life"* (John 6.63). More times than enough, some believers rely on non-spiritual words to communicate with the True and Living God whose language and Word is spiritual and eternal. When we pray the Almighty's written word, our prayers cause dynamic shifts in the universe. In the book of the Acts of the Apostles, the Bible says, *"And when they had prayed, the place where they were assembled together was shaken"* (Acts 4.31a NKJV). **As a result of praying in the Spirit, traditional and ungodly foundations are shaken and an unquestionable and unquenchable fire starts.** Never before was there such boldness for speaking God's word because there was a people who were on fire! Never before were God's people filled with this dimension of power. As you pray in the power of the Holy Spirit, you will have that same fire needed to bring down strongholds. When you pray in the power of the Holy Spirit, you are praying in a supernatural language that will unleash blessings, favor, and the plan of God to influence every aspect of your life.

The Bible says that, *"The grass withers and the flowers fade, but the Word of God stands forever."* Isaiah 40.8 NLT. **When we pray in our native language, 99.8 per cent of the time we are speaking to God by using an irrational and barren code of communication. But when we pray in the heavenly language of the Spirit we minister unto God His Word back to Him that stands forever.** There is a difference in praying prayers in the language of the Bible compared to our made-up unbiblical prayers using our native language. Two powerful ways of praying are by praying God's Word into the atmosphere, and praying in the power of the Holy Spirit. God's Word teaches that we must pray in the Spirit on all occasions.

The Power of Praying in the Heavenly Language

The language of God supersedes, exceeds, and transcends time and it is the language of heaven that transcends time, which causes us to experience miracles. Praying in the Spirit does not adjust or speed up time, but it will pierce your understanding of time and cause a synchronization of works between you and God. When you pray in the Spirit, you will not have to worry because praying with this weapon of power increases your faith and gives you peace and confidence that what you are praying for is taking place in the spirit realm. Time is not an issue for those who pray in the Spirit. In fact, your sense of time will no longer concern you because praying in the Spirit helps you to understand that in God's time there will be miracles.

Consider the revelation of Jude 1.20. *"But you, dear friends, must build each other up in your most holy faith, pray in the power of the Holy Spirit"* (Jude 1.20 NLT). We should befriend brothers and sisters in Christ who are committed to prayer and praying in the Spirit. Praying in the power of the Holy Spirit will cause you to be so confident in God's miraculous power that you will strengthen people's faith when they are discouraged, depressed, and experiencing discomfort. When you pray in the power of the Holy Spirit, your prayers will become more powerful because power is unleashed to you. When God's sons and daughters daily and painstakingly pray in the power of the Holy Spirit, they do not have to worry about anything when approaching the throne of God for prayer because they, *"Boldly come to the throne of our gracious God where they will receive the mercy of God and will find grace to help them when they need it the most."* (Hebrews 4.16 NLT)

You must know that when you go into the throne room of the King, He will grant you grace and mercy, so you will not leave His presence empty handed. But you will be equipped with everything you need and He will remove all worries, doubts, and fears. When you pray in the Spirit, you are forgiven, healed, delivered, abundant, blessed, restored, anointed, appointed, loved, faithful, developed, mature, and at the same time so much more of God's benefits are disclosed unto us. You are redefined and renewed when this spiritual awakening occurs. A greater sensitivity to His voice is enhanced in the presence of the Lord. **When we pray in the Spirit all things come into agreement with what**

God desires to be done here on earth. When we pray in the Spirit, the Kingdom of God is released in our homes, in our children, and upon our descendants to come.

From God's perspective, the most natural way to pray is in the supernatural. Praying in the Spirit is using the supernatural language of God to communicate, minister, and interact with God. Praying in God's language releases His will in our lives. Satan does not like it when we earnestly pray in the Spirit because when we have the boldness to pray in the Spirit we become unconcerned with any of life's challenges. This dimension of prayer is one of the most accurate and precise ways to pray.

There have been times when I would pray about something and I would want to quit. One morning before I started my day, I prayed to the Lord and I opened my Bible. I went to the book of Isaiah and came across Isaiah 62.7 when I was encouraged to give God no rest and pray until the Lord established His promises in my situation. If you genuinely want God to move for you, you must pray without ceasing. Our faith must get to the point where we find ourselves in dire need of submitting everything over to the Lord. We must become fed up with ordinary results and outcomes of our situations and in His power that will cause us to pray for the supernatural miracle that will be sent from the Most High God. No matter the problem, no matter the circumstance, no matter how big or small, there is nothing too difficult for God to handle.

As you pray in the Spirit, I decree that you will experience an awakening in the Spirit; that your eyes will be opened. I decree that you will be rejuvenated and refreshed to start, restart, continue, and intensify praying in the Spirit. I decree that you will pray in the power of the Spirit and you will have Divine Encounters with the Most High God. I decree that the Divine appointments with El Shaddai will be encounters you never thought you could experience in life, and that these encounters you find will be greater than this life on earth. You will grow in greater revelation about Jesus who is the Life, the Water, and the Only One who can provide the peace and comfort of the Comforter!

Oh ye of little faith!

When will healing manifest? How will I be able to begin the business? How will I make time for writing the business plan? What resource will give me the money? Am I anointed? Am I called? Why do I feel heavy? Why do I feel like God does not love me? Where is God? How come I can't feel Him? I want to know if God truly exists?

Many questions come to the surface and they hide in the shadows of our thoughts when we pray to the Lord. When we are not prayerful and not praying in the power of the Holy Spirit, 90 percent of our prayers are filled with concern, worry, doubt, and fear. **When any percentage, dimension or fraction of fear, concern, worry or doubt is wading in the thoughts concerned with what you are praying you cannot move the mountains that must be moved.** In other words, when these inhibitors are prevalent in your thoughts during prayer and even in our everyday lives, mountains will be difficult to move. Doubt is a sign of little faith. Not only is it a sign of little faith, but we reflect little faith when we do not pray in the power of the Spirit.

Do not be afraid to pray in the Spirit. Do not be concerned with the interpretation while you are privately praying in the Spirit, but have faith that your prayers are reaching the heavens. When Jesus told the disciples they were of little faith, it was normally when they were fearful, misunderstanding of the situation, and doubtful they would overcome the trial they faced. They became fearful when the wind increased its velocity and the waves climbed heights they had never experienced. **When they became fearful, they were hindered in performing the works of Christ. Read these words carefully: When you become fearful, consumed in your feelings, and doubtful, you are hindered in performing the works of Christ.**

It is absolutely normal to feel discouraged and suddenly cease praying in the Spirit. There have been many occasions when I have gotten discouraged and ceased praying. I remember a time when I thought my prayers were not getting through and I stopped praying in my heavenly language. I did not stop for a few days either, but I stopped for weeks. When I stopped praying in the Spirit, I changed to another mode of prayer during that time. I went from praying in the Spirit to sitting in the presence of the Lord while I listened to Him speak to me. I will elaborate more about sitting in His presence in the chapter entitled, "Be Still." But when I quietly sat in the presence of the Lord, I received a word of confirmation from the Lord saying, *"You've prayed in the power of God the Holy Spirit for some time. I am taking you to a deeper place of faith when you pray in the power of the Spirit. I am going to increase and advance your understanding about praying in the Spirit."* When you pray in the power of the Spirit, the Holy Spirit will speak to you to get you ready to perform and experience miracles and feats in the name of Jesus. You will be victorious. Just have faith in knowing that when you pray in the Spirit, strongholds will be torn down, demons will retaliate, but the power of the Holy Spirit will give you the power to fight the enemy. Pray in the Spirit, and listen to the voice of the Lord! As you pray in the Spirit, pause to hear what the Lord will say. You will hear the Holy Spirit confirm things to you that were told to you in times past. Hear His voice as you pray in the power of the Spirit and you will be at peace. When the Lord shared His heart with me about praying in the power of the Spirit, it made me overwhelmed with confidence and excitement to pray in the Spirit more. I immediately started praying in the Spirit with great intensity.

We should become joyful when God speaks to us because it confirms His love for us. We hold ourselves in such high standards and sometimes our standards can be abusive and contrary to the mercy, long-suffering, and grace of God. I've witnessed people stone themselves for mistakes they have made, and the stones have caused people to cease praying. The Holy Spirit will minister to you about a certain issue and chastise you because of His unfailing love. Believe that you are forgiven and forgive yourself. Do not throw stones at yourself because by throwing stones you will eventually take away your own life. Stand in awe of God, because His love never ends.

The Holy Spirit ministered this word to me during a night in prayer and He said, *"I did not lose hope in you nor have I given up on you, but you have given up on yourself and lost hope in the love I promised you."* God continuously reminds me that His love suffers long. So when God shares

His heart with you, you can be overjoyed because it's an indication that He never breaks a promise.

A long time ago I learned that God never leaves us, but we leave Him; and He is waiting with open arms for us to come back to Him. There are some lessons the Lord wants to teach you about praying in the Spirit. One important lesson I already shared, which is to never doubt, question, and become fearful about what you are saying while praying in the power of the Spirit; and just know your prayers are kissing heaven. The second lesson is that when you pray in the Spirit you are releasing healing, deliverance, salvation, restoration, and miracles into the world, nations, your country, state, and city, local church, family, and you are also releasing protection to yourself personally.

Another aspect of praying in the Spirit I have not mentioned yet is that we must always pray in the Spirit when engaging in spiritual warfare. In fact, when we pray in the Spirit, we are engaging ourselves in dismantling the weapons of Satan and the various areas the enemy is hiding. The Holy Spirit will show you attacks that are coming and where the enemy will hide. The Holy Spirit will bring you to the battleground to fight and destroy the garrisons the enemy has built. A garrison is a fort that troops build in order to prevent their enemy from gaining more ground and territory than what has already been gained. Garrisons of opposition arise when we find ourselves committed to praying in the Spirit, but for some reason we abruptly stop. Spiritual garrisons stops the enemy in his tracks and it is the same when you stop praying in the Spirit; the enemy attempts to stop you in your tracks. You must plow through every demonic garrison the enemy builds so you can gain more ground when it comes to praying. Do not walk in fear, and do not be alarmed when this happens because the Lord will strategically position angels at certain places to stop the enemy in his tracks. There have been many times when I thought my prayers were not reaching the heavens, but continuing to pray in the Spirit will cause your faith to increase and rid yourself from worrying about discouragement. Satan attempts to cause us to believe we are rotten sinners. Satan likes it when we make promises to God and we break those promises. Each time we submit ourselves to self-condemnation, guilt, and shame, we fail to pray in the Spirit, which causes us to discount ourselves from feeling worthy and powerful enough to pray in the Spirit. These examples are oppositional garrisons. Do not allow the enemy to tell you that you are no longer a man or woman of God. Do not allow the enemy tell you that you are not a true prayer warrior. **Intimacy is not broken when we cease to pray in the Spirit. When we speak the language of God, our intimacy with Him is unified and on one accord. We begin to speak what the Holy Spirit speaks, and glorify our Mighty King Jesus. So pray more in the power of the Holy Spirit and don't quit!**

I will never forget when I first became intimate with Christ. I was sleeping and the Holy Spirit awakened me. I got on my knees to pray to the Almighty God. The next thing I knew, I was interacting with God in a manner which I never experienced. I did not say, "Hallelujah" or, "Thank you Jesus." I felt fire and tears of joy be released from my eyes. I heard a sound come from my voice that had never been released before. I did not know what I said, but I knew I was communicating with the Father by the power of the

Holy Spirit. No one ever laid hands on me, and no one ever shouted in my ear to tell me what to say. But I heard the sound of heaven and I spoke to the Father in His language, and I saw, in the spirit, a pathway being opened for me. The Holy Spirit took me to a spiritual place of new beginnings that would afford me to experience new natural beginnings. Ever since that early morning encounter I could not stop praying in the Spirit. The more you pray in the Spirit, the more you will notice that your hunger for what is unholy will be totally annihilated. I pray that you will fall in love with praying in the Spirit because it is the way to give all glory to the Lord.

There is no need to live in the guilt and shame of sin. There is no longer a concern with what you are doing or not doing that is right or wrong. The days of achieving endeavors and accomplishing feats with the reliance of your personal power have been put to an end. It's time to utilize the power of the Holy Spirit. It's time to rely on God's power, His will, and His plan for your life!

Because praying in the Spirit is praying in the heavenly language of God, the Holy Spirit will begin to show you things in the Spirit. As the Almighty Holy Spirit shows you events in the Spirit, the Holy Spirit will begin to heavily influence your thoughts and speech. Praying in the Spirit will supernaturally compel you to neglect the desire and unconscious need to satisfy the flesh.

Since I have been praying in the Spirit, the ministry that the Lord has given me has become more saturated with the presence of EL Shaddai. Because He is the Great I AM, there is no greater presence I could possibly want than the presence of EL Shaddai. The Lord Almighty transforms the personality that has been influenced by media, school, parents, and so on, to His personality. **I pray in the Spirit because I need the persona of the Almighty King, the Anointed One, our Lord Jesus Christ.** As I pray, I see in the Spirit, and meditate in the Spirit. All things are covered when we pray in the power of the Holy Spirit. If we pray daily in the power of the Holy Spirit, the Almighty King will honor your faith and bless every spiritual interaction you experience with Him. Try to establish a daily meeting time with God. When you are present for your divine appointment with the Almighty God, the sound of your voice will be heard in the realm of the Spirit, and the Son of God will know you are honoring His presence. He will show you things that are going to happen in the earth and in your life. Pay close attention for the preview of God showing His rule and reign over heaven and earth.

Praying in the Spirit = Greater Faith; Greater Faith = Greater Works

Praying in the power of the Holy Spirit is so powerful that God rewards those who do so because this level of earnestness ushers in the presence of the Lord over our lives. *"Without faith, it is impossible to please God; those that come to God must believe that He is God, and that He is a rewarder of those who diligently seek Him."* (Hebrews 11.6 NKJV)

When the Hebrews left Egypt to follow Moses into the land of Promise, they did not have any clue as to where they were going, but they followed Moses anyway. What I find interesting is the means in which they travelled. When the Hebrews initially left Egypt they thought they were better off remaining in Egypt until the Egyptian army chased them and the Red Sea was ahead of the Hebrews. The Hebrews had a few options which were either to:

1. Commit suicide,

2. Stop running and be brought back into slavery or killed, or

3. Run into the Red Sea hoping they would swim through the waters.

Either way, all three of these options could have allowed the Hebrews to ultimately die in some way, shape, or form. Instead of committing suicide and resubmitting their lives to Pharaoh, the Hebrews decided to trust the Almighty. The Israelites despised living in bondage to the Egyptians so much that they risked not knowing where their journey would bring them as they veered closer to the Red Sea. Before I continue, please understand: **praying in the power of the Holy Spirit is for believers that desire to no longer be in bondage to anything any longer.** The Hebrews knew they should follow Moses as Moses received his direction from God, because of the Almighty's promise of passing over every door that was covered with the blood. The Hebrews leaving Egypt spoke volumes when it came to their faith because they did not have to continue going all the way when they approached the Red Sea.

When the Hebrews arrived to the Red Sea they did not quit running, but they continued all the way through and they literally watched their enemy become swallowed by the waters of the Red Sea. Because of the Hebrews' faith, they literally watched the Almighty God create a pathway of escape for them to travel through the Red Sea. The Almighty

God created this pathway by splitting the waters in such a way they would be like walls of water to the left and right of the Hebrews. The Almighty held up the waters on both sides until the Chosen people of the Almighty would have gotten to the other side of the Red Sea. The faith of the Chosen people enabled them to receive a miracle, escape re-entering bondage, and watch their enemy be swallowed in the Red Sea.

Approaching the Red Sea is what I think praying in the power of the Holy Spirit can be like. I know the Almighty requires us to pray in the Spirit, but to be honest, sometimes my mind is not satisfied and I do not feel so secure, as opposed to when I pray in my native language. We should never see prayer as a remedy to make us feel good, but when we pray, our spirit should be strengthened. It is easy to feel secure when praying in your native language and that is a real feeling. However, praying in the power of the Spirit spiritually protects you. Later on, the Lord told me that the feelings I had derived from fear and uncertainty, but I now believe that through my faith I am moving mountains and creating an environment for God's presence to move in supernatural and miraculous ways. It takes a great level of faith to approach the Red Sea, but it takes a higher level of faith to continue to walk through the sea as God divides the waters for you to journey safely. Pray in the Spirit and experience God divide waters for you to safely and smoothly walk through the waters.

When I first started to seriously pray in the power of the Holy Spirit, I prayed in this manner because I wanted to be obedient to the Word of God. At first, I did not know what would come of it, nor did I know in what direction my prayer journeyed. I also did not feel secure. When I prayed in my native language, I felt like I covered all of my bases because I could understand and hear myself pray for foreign nations, my family, the ministry, my job, my wife, and I interceded for other people's situations as well. As I continued to be faithful to praying in the power of the Holy Spirit, I noticed a peace that truly surpassed all understanding. I learned that praying in the Spirit released the fruit of the Spirit in my character. I no longer worried about things and did not become overwhelmed with the thought of, "What if this prayer does not get answered?" **Praying in the Spirit will take you out of the bondage of doubt, and release you into the land of great faith and spiritual power!** Some are a little skeptical about forfeiting native language prayers for praying in the heavenly language of the Almighty God, but **praying in tongues is our native language**! We are not of this world, but **we are heavenly citizens required to speak in the language of heaven. When we pray in the Spirit, we are advancing God's will for the earth as it is in heaven.**

It is not too often one can travel to a nation and expect to communicate clearly in one's own native language. The same principle applies when communicating with the Almighty God. **We cannot sit in heavenly places and expect to use our authority on earth by praying in the language, knowledge, and wisdom of the world.**

Praying in the power of the Almighty prepares us for spiritual battles. It is not a coincidence that the apostle Paul tells the church to "pray in the Spirit on all occasions" to further outline what the church wrestles against in the realm of the Spirit. Whenever we pray in the Spirit, we put on our warfare armor and we utilize our armor and weapons. Because we pray in the Spirit, we serve the enemy its pre-eviction notice on wherever Satan seeks to make his abode. Every battle is won when we pray in the Spirit. Signs, wonders, and miracles are outcomes of praying in the Spirit.

The fact that we pray in the power of the Almighty strengthens our native language. As a result of praying in the Spirit we believe our own decrees and declarations according to the word of God. We develop a praying spirit and then we can ask God for anything and He will release it into our lives and situations. **The heavenly language informs, influences, and empowers our earthen language.** Remember, when we pray in the power of the Holy Spirit, we pray God's will to be done on earth as it is in heaven. Therefore, everything on earth becomes better as a result of praying in the power of the Spirit.

There are two things the Lord would want us to understand about praying in the Spirit: 1. Whoever practices praying in the Spirit is a mortal attempting to connect with our Immortal Heavenly Father, and mortals will become stronger in the Spirit, and 2. The enemy does not want any of God's people to commit to praying in the Spirit because their eyes will become opened to the power of El Shaddai. In addition, the enemy's influences will become weakened. However, the enemy will not discontinue his attacks.

When I learned these things, I picked up my weapons of warfare of praying in the Spirit. I recommitted my prayer life to praying in the Spirit and I prayed with more intensity and with greater faith. I started to cast out demons, heal the sick, and raise the dead in the name of Jesus. You will do greater works because you believe with great faith that you are tapping into the awesome presence of God.

The Language of Glory

As I started to pray, the Lord told me to re-read Psalms 19.1 that states, *"The heavens declare the glory of God"*(Psalm 19.1 NKJV). And when I started praying the Lord affirmed the revelation knowledge that the heavens speak of God's glory. In other words, the heavenly language is the language of glory. When we pray in the language of heaven, we are praying in the language of glory and in the glory of God. While we pray in the glory language, we begin to release God's glory from out of our heart into the earth. The glory of God's language begins to fill the room and His glory arises. Let the glory of the Lord rise unto El Shaddai! **May your heart meet and become intimate with the Glory of heaven.**

For there has never been a stronger and greater generation as this generation to ever touch the earth, nor will there ever be a generation like this generation. There have been thousands of generations, but this generation is different because it has a different type of genetic landscape. *Genus* (s) and *genera* (pl.) was used during the 1550s as a term of logic that meant "kind or class of things." When used in biological settings, dating from 1660, the Latin word *genus* was a term associated with "race, stock, kind; family, birth, descent, origin," cognate with the Greek word *genos* "race, kind." *Gonos* is another Greek word, which means "birth, offspring, stock;" all deriving from the root **gene*, which means "produce, give birth, beget," with derivatives referring to

44

family and tribal groups. The Latin word *gignere* means "to beget," and *gnasci* "to be born." The Latin word *genius* means "procreative divinity, inborn tutelary spirit, innate quality." The Bible in Joel 2.2b says that, *"A people come, great and strong, the like of whom has never been; nor will there ever be any such after them, even for many successive generation."* You must believe you are the generation that is filled and baptized with the Holy Spirit that will never touch the earth again. It is our time to really tap into the heart of God and experience His signs, wonders, and miracles. This is the time of power! This is the time the Lord wants to, unlike any time before, move and operate through God's people to shake the earth with His word.

The Language that Sounds the Alarm

During ancient times, warriors and soldiers always knew when to prepare for battle because of the sounding of the alarm. Whenever Navy ships approach danger, a loud alarming noise is made to notify the Navy soldiers that they must prepare for war. However, every soldier, regardless of division, whether he or she may be in the Army, Navy, Marine, or the Airforce, these soldiers are always on guard. It is their duty to be alert at all times because they understand that the enemy can strike at any time. Not only are they aware that the enemy can attack at any time, they are certain that there is an enemy against the United States. The first agreement a prayer warrior must realize is that Satan and Satan's angels are the enemy. In addition, anything that opposes God's Word, His Truth, and His chosen is the enemy.

After the prayer warrior understands that Satan is the enemy, one must realize that Satan can attack at anytime, any place, and anyhow. There is no need to be afraid or paranoid, but this does mean that every saved person in Christ Jesus must always be alert and on guard. In fact, warfare is always taking place. The enemy will attack your wife, your husband, your finances, your health, your mind, your colleagues and co-workers, family members, your children, and everything else you interact with on a daily basis. In fact, I believe one of the easiest and most vulnerable areas the enemy attacks first are our minds. The attack against some individuals' minds is the skepticism about praying in the Spirit and all of the other designated terms I'm using to describe and explain praying in the Spirit. Some of the thoughts that invade people's minds are: "I don't have to pray in the Spirit," and "I don't know what I'm praying for and against," and "I'm releasing witchcraft curses," and "Praying and speaking in tongues have ceased" and "I do not believe this is real" and "I sinned last night and I feel defeated," and "I don't feel 'powerful enough' to pray in the Spirit because that's only for confident, powerful men and women of God," and "I'm not a pastor or leader in the church so why should I go deeper in faith and pray in the Spirit?" Now some of these examples are invitations for the enemy to give you answers and some of the other examples are skeptical thoughts of deception that the enemy wants you to reason in your mind as to why you should *not* pray in the Spirit. These thoughts and examples are the beginning of the warfare. In fact, because these ideas may be surfacing your mind, you should begin praying in the Spirit now to defeat the infiltration of the powers, principalities, rulers of darkness of this age, and spiritual wickedness in heavenly places.

Whenever we pray in the Spirit, about anything, we wear down the enemy. We overload and make the burden too heavy for the enemy to carry out its plan.

So the alarm is the sound of heaven being released from your voice box, located in your throat and your tongue. The Bible teaches us that "the tongue can bring death or life" (Proverbs 18.21 NKJV). The enemy can hear the alarm and the sound of the language of glory is so powerful that it is similar to the sound of praise. This means praying in the Spirit should come from a place when one is pure at heart, and this purity of heart causes the enemy to hear the alarm and flee. In fact, the sound of the Spirit causes the enemy to stand down. In other words, the enemy drops its weapons and flees. When the sound of glory is released the enemy becomes powerless and weak. In fact, like our praise, the language of glory confuses, irritates, and frustrates the works of the enemy. To simplify this idea further, Satan and his angels become extremely mad. **We can always count ourselves victorious when we pray in the Spirit** because Satan and his angels drops its weapons and flees, but waits for you to become weak in your faith to re-attack you.

We do not wrestle against flesh and blood (people, physicality), but against principalities (ranking demons), powers (spiritual authorities), rulers of darkness of the age (evil spirits), and against spiritual wickedness in heavenly places (fallen angels). Why are we trying to wage war in the spirit realm using a man-made language? It is apparent in the Scriptures that we must "always pray in the Spirit" in order to be victorious in a spiritual battle. When a person steps up to the podium during a battle of debates, the debater never speaks in the heavenly language, but he or she debates in the chosen man-made language. Why? Because the debate is a battle of intelligence and human knowledge; and it is not a spiritual battle. **If you want to win the spiritual battle, pray in the Spirit!**

CHAPTER IV

Be Still

"But the Lord said to her, 'My Dear Martha, you are worried and upset over all these details! There is only one thing worth being concerned about. Mary has discovered it, and it will not be taken away from her.'" (Luke 10.42 NLT)

One of the greatest benefits of communicating is truly listening to someone talk with 100 percent focus and attention. What I appreciate most about people who share their problems with me is the inability I have to solve them, but having the understanding and ability to listen to them solve their own problems by allowing them to listen to themselves talk. When people are given the opportunity to talk they are sometimes able to think clearly and deeply about what exactly they are experiencing and saying that causes them to receive greater understanding about how to resolve their issue. So when people call me for advice, I don't say a word until they ask me a question. This usually happens after they have been talking (and I have been listening) for about 15-20 minutes; sometimes even up to 45 minutes.

Another benefit of listening to people talk is that I am then able to understand the true essence of that person's problem and challenge. I can then ask the right questions causing them to figure out their problems by themselves, without any suggestions from me. After I have asked the person a few questions and they have figured out what to do, most frequently they end the conversation with, "Thank you. You were a big help." And I think to myself, "I didn't suggest or recommend anything to you, yet you're thanking me?" The reality is that they are thanking me because I know how to listen.

The reason why God is such a wonderful counselor is because He listens to us when we pray. God rarely interrupts me while speaking to Him during prayer. The reason why I believe we feel so great after prayer is because God is a great listner. We could have prayed for everything under the sun according to His will, and we say Amen while He says Amen! After we say Amen, we are joyful and we thank Jesus for all He has done for us. Meanwhile, Jesus is sitting on His throne smiling as we praise His name.

But have you realized that the Lord has to get some things off of His chest as well? The Holy Spirit has a lot to share with us that we sometimes miss during prayer because we do all of the talking. The worst counseling sessions are the sessions when the counselor dominates the conversation and you do not have the chance to get anything off of your chest. The next thing you know, your hour-long session is over and it was not productive for you. Most of the time this results in no peace, joy, vision or direction. As a result you feel like your time was wasted. In the same way, I humbly believe your time is wasted when you dominate your prayer time with saying so many things to the Lord, while He is sitting on His throne waiting for you to allow Him to speak. He will allow you to go on and on without saying a word.

I am certain we experience times when driving our car, we stop at a red light, and the Holy Spirit will send us a message that has something to do with what is happening down the road and He'll tell us, through a whisper, to take a detour. However, since we are not accustomed to giving God a chance to share His insight during our personal prayer time by listening to His voice, we get to that roadwork ahead, and say to ourselves, "Something told me to take a detour!" Well my dear brothers and sisters, that was not "something' that told you to take a detour. That was the Holy Spirit telling you there was a roadblock ahead and you need to take the detour now in order to save time later.

After attending church for more than twenty years no one had ever emphasized to me the importance of hearing the voice of the Lord. However, it's one of the most important lessons I feel we can learn. I am grateful to God because I have since learned how important it is to hear God's voice. Psalm 119.105 says, *Your word is a lamp to my feet and a light to my path.* God speaks His word to us that is like a burning fire, as a hammer that breaks the rock in pieces. (Jeremiah 23.29) His word is living and powerful; sharper than any two-edged sword, and it pierces swiftly and deeply even to the division of the soul and spirit, and of joints and marrow, and it is also a discerner of the intents of the heart. There are so many wonderful qualities and aspects of listening to God speak and share His word, but how are you to live without hearing? The reason why it is important to hear His word during prayer is because you must understand His perspective through His lens. His word is the guide that your feet needs in order to walk in the right direction, and the light that makes your paths clear and easy to see exactly where you are walking. God will never allow you to walk alone because He promised to never leave you nor forsake you. He is the light of the world and in Him there is no darkness. This is why it is important to hear His voice because He will help you to see and understand things from a pure perspective. When God speaks, He will save you and prevent you from journeying down wrongful paths. Your understanding of prayer must arrive to the place where you are comfortable remaining quiet while you listen to Him speak. It may feel strange the first few times you sit in silence, but be confident that the Lord is speaking to you at all times, and your ear and spirit is developed during those quiet times.

Be still, says the Lord, and know that I am God! These words never meant much to me when I was 12 years old as I heard the Choral Choir sing a hymn called "Be Still And Know that I AM God" during prayer on Sundays. This hymn put me to sleep because the choir sung it as if it were a dirge, which sung me to a peaceful sleep during service. About three years ago, "be still" began to have greater meaning in my prayer life.

"Be still" is a command from the Lord, teaching us to have no worries, no distractions, no doubts, and to be calm while in His presence. Being still means to not move but it means to remove the busy work and sit with the confidence that God is present. Being still and knowing that God is present is a great move of faith because you must believe that the Lord is actually with you. Not only do you have to believe that God is present, but you have to believe that God exists. If you do not believe that God exists, then you cannot be still and know that He is God. If God does not exist then there is no point in being still. So it is in our stillness that we can begin to practice listening to the voice of the Lord. This is a teaching vital to the life of God's people, as is meditating on His word day and night. If you meditate on God's decrees, laws, teachings, instructions, and words day and night, you will be like a tree that is planted by the rivers of living water that brings forth fruit in its season. Your leaf will not wither but whatever you do will prosper! You are called to prosper and prosperity is the plan for your life!

The word *meditate* is used fourteen times in the King James Version and the word *meditation* six times. Just because the word *meditation* is not used as much as the word *pray* does not mean it is something Christians should overlook. Meditation is the most major part with God's word coming alive in your life. There are many people who doubt God, and they need God's word to come alive in their lives. Because they have not meditated on His word, it has yet to come alive in their lives.

Abraham's wealth was passed down by inheritance to Isaac, Abraham's son. It was so important for Isaac to be married to a special woman that Abraham sent his servant to search for Isaac's wife based on an oath. Abraham's servant wanted to succeed at Abraham's oath so much that he prayed to the Lord to grant him success on this mission of finding Isaac's wife. Needless to say, Abraham's servant was successful with finding Isaac's wife, Rebekah, and when the servant was on his way back to their land with her, the Bible says, *"Isaac was walking and meditating in the fields."* Verse 63 of chapter 24 in Genesis says that when Isaac opened his eyes he saw camels coming toward him and his bride was riding on top of one of those camels. When

Isaac and Rebekah met each other it was love at first sight. Rebekah was such a gift from the Lord that she brought Isaac comfort after his mother died. Genesis 24 is one of the stories that proves to me that nothing but good can happen as a result of meditating. In this context, the word *meditation* means to muse, and muse means to become absorbed in thought, especially to turn something over in the mind often inconclusively. The Bible says Isaac meditated, which was probably a practice he learned from his father of great faith. God is so calculated that He knows what we need and when we need it, and as such He will always grant our heart's desires at the divinely appointed time. God gave Rebekah to Isaac shortly before Sarah, his mother, died. God gave Isaac a wife at just the right time. And likewise, God will give you what you need at just the right time. You will receive the favor and blessings that the Lord has for you when you begin to envision what God wants for you. Start meditating on what God says to Jeremiah, "For I know the thought that I think toward you, says the Lord, thoughts of peace and not of evil, to give you a future and a hope. Then you will call upon Me and go and pray to Me, and I will listen to you." (Jeremiah 29.11,12 NKJV) Meditate on this word and watch God show you the things to come. And when you open your eyes, God will unleash blessings into your hands, your lap, and into everything connected to your life.

The Lord admonishes Joshua to meditate on the law day and night and promises that if he does this he will experience success. Meditation causes us to practice diligence and it teaches us how to be focused on what God wants to do through us on the earth. You must understand

and believe that your purpose on the earth is bigger than your problems, short-comings, and mistakes. What God has planned for you must be completed through the means of prayer. **Your life depends on prayer and failing to meditate on His promises will cause great harm for you and humanity!** I do not believe people understand the sincerity of what I'm saying as it relates to their purpose and humanity. I admonish you to begin praying now to tap in to the character and nature of Christ so that when the Lord brings you before nations to prophesy, pray, minister, heal, and everything else you are called to do, you will (re)present Christ to the world.

God's plans for Joshua and Jeremiah were for them to prosper. Your plans to prosper are the same plans the Lord desires for you as well. Meditation is a major factor of this dimension of prayer. The person that delights themselves in the decrees of the Lord is blessed.

> *"Blessed is the man that walketh not in the counsel of the ungodly nor standeth in the way of sinners, nor sitteth in the seat of the scornful. But his delight is in the law of the Lord; and in His law doeth he meditate day and night. And he shall be like a tree that is planted by the rivers of water that bringeth forth fruit in its season; and his leaves shall not wither, but whatsoever he doeth shall PROSPER!*
> Psalm 1.1-3

Everything that is good will result from meditating on what God says to you. When I prepare to minister God's word to His people, I do not write sermons and addresses, but I quiet my spirit and sit before the Lord listening to His voice. Once I hear God speak, I write down what God says, and then I meditate on His decrees. As I hear God speak, He guides me to the Scriptures that confirms His word, and peace erupts in my nervous system causing me to stand and speak before God's people without fear. The Scriptures teach us that we profit and prosper from meditating. And Jesus said to Martha, "Mary had discovered it!" (Luke 10.42 NLT)

Mary is sitting at the feet of Jesus and Martha is busy preparing a special dinner for Jesus because she thinks Jesus is impressed with presentation as opposed to Jesus being impressed with us presenting our ears to His voice. Jesus is talking to Mary, and Martha becomes frustrated because Martha is concerned with impressing Jesus with a delightful meal while Mary is quietly listening to Jesus teach her. Jesus tells Martha that Mary has the revelation and Martha does not have the revelation.

Jesus is not saying that Martha should not prepare dinner, but He is saying that Martha does not have the right mindset about being in His presence. Mary's mindset teaches us that Jesus is concerned with us being attentive and reverent in His presence rather than what we can do or say to impress Him. When we revere His presence, we are then able to sit still and know that He is the Creator of the Universe and He is the Ruler over all. When we understand that God is the Commander of the things that have been spoken into being, we are then able to receive instruction from Him because His wisdom is infinite.

There is this pervasive idea that busy-ness means productivity and achievement. I write this to let you know that if you believe this you have it all wrong as it comes to being busy. **God has never called us to be busy, but He has called us to be still!** Miracles stem from this level of intimacy with God. When we muse over the things God says, we are thinking about the Word non-stop. Jesus is the Word and the Word was spoken into existence. Meditation breeds deep thought and concern for something, so when we meditate on the Word we are giving deep thought and concern for the nature and character of Jesus Christ. There is a song that states, "Down at your feet O Lord is the Most High Place in Your presence Lord, I seek Your face." And then it says, "There is no higher calling, no greater honor than to bow and kneel before Your throne!" People of God, this is what Mary did. She kneeled at the feet of the Lord and God found her act of reverence to be honorable. And of all the people attempting to impress Jesus, Mary had discovered the missing component to hearing the heart of the Lord. If we could remove ourselves from every distraction and everything that steals our time away from God, we would prosper in whatever we do.

CHAPTER V

Expect Divine Encounters

"Without any real encounter with God, there is no genuine faith in the impossible made possible"

Expect a divine encounter with the Lord and from His angelic armies and messengers of heaven. I recall many encounters with God and many angelic visitations, which often caught me off guard. The encounters I have experienced were not because of my righteousness and even unrighteousness; but He graced me with these encounters because of His love. In fact, my first encounter was life changing and I will never forget it. It happened before the turn of 2007, and during that time I was in no spiritual shape to have "deserved" such a visitation. The visitation happened after a late night hanging out with my best friend, Carson. Carson and I were not thinking about being devoted to God, we did not have any spiritual discussion, nor were we seeking God to intervene in our lives. We were in our mid-twenties and we were young and free. Our decision-making skills were not exercised in some situations, but we did have a moral compass that directed how we wanted to be publicly perceived.

When Carson and I hung out that night, we stayed out until about 1:00 a.m. and then I went home to bed. Somewhere between 1:00-3:50 I had dreamed of seven candle lit lamp stands in a dark room, which lit the room enough to see what was in there. I was not concerned with what was in the room, but I knew only two things:

1.) it was only God and I in the room, and

2.) there was a deep and soothing voice that spoke and immediately comforted me.

The voice behind the seven candle lit lamp stands said, *"I am calling you to live for me to minister to many people; you cannot do what you want, but I will protect and provide for you as you live for Me!"* At the time, my plans were to be an Intellectual Property Lawyer in Los Angeles, California. My additional plans were to party and rub shoulders with celebrities as we helped each other make millions of dollars. I wanted to complete contracts for many famous musical artists, and to be the "Johnny Cochran" of entertainment. The encounter was so powerful that an angel came to me and told me to worship the Lord. I woke up at about 4:00 a.m. and I knelt in front of my bed and stretched out my arms toward heaven. I opened the palms of my hands and the next thing you know, I started to communicate to the Lord in a language I'd never spoken before, and I cried out to the Lord.

Although it took me about six months to understand that dream and encounter, I did not give it any thought that morning. However, from that day on nothing seemed to work out for me the way I planned. Not only did my plans fail, but I started viewing my actions differently. I felt bad about the activities I engaged in and I started to find myself alone in parks staring into heaven. I would bring my Bible with me and read God's Word when I should have been studying for the law program courses.

While I was taking these law courses I was given an assignment to write a paper on what I planned on accomplishing in the legal field. I wrote that I wanted to close down liquor stores because they caused poverty and violence. I also wrote that I wanted to feed the hungry and give away clothes to people who were less fortunate. Looking back on that paper, I realize that I could have been a Social Justice lawyer, but at that time Social Justice was not an interest of mine. Interestingly enough, I did not give Intellectual Property law a second guess; I simply submitted the paper hoping for an 'A.' Besides the grammatical errors in the paper, the content was alarming for my professor and he wrote a note at the top of the paper that said, "Let's talk!" I was amazed because he had not given me a grade for my effort. So I scheduled a meeting with him during his office hours and he told me that my future goals did not align with those of most lawyers who journey into the Intellectual Property field of law. He told me I should attend seminary because he believed my life had a different purpose. I was crushed at that moment because I knew that what he told me aligned with what God wanted me to do as it related to receiving further understanding about faith. Nevertheless, I took his advice and finished the semester at the school of law and enrolled into seminary. From the day the professor and I had that conversation, I've been devoted to prayer. I spent many days, sometimes months, praying and fasting and seeking the face of God, and as I did this I had some interesting encounters. The Lord gave me visions of thousands of people lain out in worship to His Holy name. I received visions of people being healed, and I jumped into studying God's word with greater hunger for who God is and what He had done throughout history. My interest grew in God so much that I wanted to understand how people like Jesus would be so obedient, Elijah's encounters with God, and the Apostle Paul's zeal to spread the gospel of Jesus Christ.

I will never forget how Saul was on his way to Damascus riding on a donkey, but I also learned how violent he was before he had a Divine encounter. He was so violent that he would kill Christians. One day he heard a voice come from heaven and he was instantly blinded. As I read the story, a prophet came to him and took him in and told him that if he did not submit to the Lord Jesus Christ he would remain blind. Saul agreed to submit, and a couple of things happened: 1.) the scales that blinded Saul fell off his eyes, and 2.) his name was changed to Paul. I marveled at this story because Paul had an encounter with God that literally changed everything in his life. Not only did his name change, but his reputation changed and people could not believe that Paul was a brand new person. His name changed from Saul to Paul because God gave Him a new heart that would precede godly character. Paul did not learn about Christ on his own but prophets and men of God tutored him on the salvation of Jesus Christ. His hunger to know more about the salvation of Jesus Christ skyrocketed so much that he believed he had to share this salvation story with the world. Paul presented himself out of deference to the apostle Peter and other apostles and they dispatched him to be the apostle to the Gentiles whom were a people considered not worthy to come near to God. Everything changed and nothing was the same as it had been in the past. God made everything new for Paul. The Divine encounters you have with God will be life changing! They will bring in a newness and freshness of life that will make your paths straight. You will not only be a new person, but your reputation will be renewed, too. You will be so fired up that you will not be able to remain silent. You will be like Jeremiah, on fire to the point you will heal the sick and perform exploits for the glory of God!

Divine encounters cause us to supernaturally come into alignment with the will of the Father. One thing I learned about my first Divine encounter was that no matter how long I ignored God for and by not responding with action, nothing would go right in my life. When we respond with a no, things will not be favorable for us. But when we respond with a yes and our actions follow our "yes," things fall into place for us that are favorable. Divine encounters can be so overwhelming because you can experience them at any time during the day or night.

I recall on many occasions when I went to bed after reading the Bible, and during the night the Lord would send an angel to wake me up to receive a message from the Lord. I can also remember being so stubborn that I would go back and forth with an angel because I wanted to go back to sleep. Usually when an angel wakes me during the middle of the night, or during the early hours of the morning, I begin to pray in the Spirit. At this stage in my understanding of God, I no longer pray in the Spirit, but I remain silent and listen to the message the Lord wants me to hear unless He tells me otherwise. I now understand that when a messenger awakens me that is sent by the Lord, I know there must be something the Lord wants me to know.

Divine encounters are great because they will prepare you for what the Lord will do in your life. Because of these encounters, you can expect to be given unexplainable favor, to engage the kingdom of darkness in spiritual warfare, miracles, and greater levels of wisdom, knowledge, and understanding about some aspect of life. Not only do great things happen as a result of Divine encounters, but when you have them be confident in knowing that something transformational is on its way into your life: family, relationships, job, ministry, anointing, and everything else connected to you.

I am certain that you have had many encounters with God, and I pray you do not overlook them or write them off as something unimportant to your relationship with God. Even as you read this chapter about encounters with God, I pray you reflect back to the moments you had with the Lord when He told you and showed you something amazing. If you ignored His message, go back to it and pray to the Lord that He will bring that encounter back to your memory so you can begin living in greater understanding, knowledge, and wisdom. If you do remember the encounters you had with God, but have not accepted what God wants for you, tap into the plan of God for your life. Be alert! Elijah was very alert when he journeyed to Mt. Sinai because when the earthquake, fire, and wind passed by him, he knew that God was not speaking; but God spoke in a still small voice. We must be alert and open to the simple manner in which God decides to speak to us. Elijah had an encounter with

God that literally changed the trajectory of his ministry. God wanted Elijah to go on to greater dimensions in God and it took him to be alone and alert to know when God spoke and what God wanted him to do. You must also know what God wants to do in your life. Prayer will cause you to prosper in ministry because you will receive the instruction and insight from God about how to live for Him.

Jacob's faith was so deeply rooted in the Almighty that he would wake up in the morning and God would randomly send an angel to meet him. Jacob was aware that no matter what occurred in his life, he knew God was concerned with him. I am writing this to let you know that God is concerned about you and everything that surrounds your life. Just as Jesus was concerned about the Gentile woman in Matthew 15.21-28, who socially had no right to speak with a Jewish man, her worship and faith in Christ Jesus actually healed her daughter of the demonic influence. God's concern for Jacob was so great that God would wake Jacob in the morning, and he knew that angels had been sent by God to meet him (Genesis 32.1). You must know and believe that God is forever with you because He is concerned with every aspect of your life. **God wants you to be aware of His affiliation with you. Do you realize that your awareness of God's faithful presence and influence in your life can bring about healing in your body? Just being aware of God can bring about favor in your daily endeavors; just being aware of God can make your life fully peaceful, and the distractions that cause you to become frustrated will no longer bother you the way they had in the past.** God does not want you to worry about things that may frustrate you because they can cause you to lose focus of your life's purpose.

It may not seem like your thoughts are encompassed with God's plan for your life, but God has affiliated His plan with your life. If you allow God to take over your life, your ministry, your marriage, and your relationship with the person who seems to be against you for whatever reason, you will witness God turn the tables. **God will turn tables around and sit you in a seat of favor.**

In Genesis chapters 28-35, Jacob has amazing and life-changing encounters with God. One day Jacob decided to rest in Beth'el and when he fell asleep, he dreamed that the heavens opened and angels were ascending and descending the stairway. God appeared to Jacob and promised him that He would not leave him until He had finished giving him everything. That same endurance, faithfulness, and long-suffering God had for Jacob, God also has for you. God will finish what He starts. **He is a God of completion!**

When Jacob woke up he said, "Surely the Lord is in this place and I was not even aware of it." Jacob called Beth'el the gateway to heaven, but not only was Luz, now called Beth'el, the gateway to heaven, but everyone, from that point onward, would have known that Beth'el is the place where this revelation was discovered: **that there is unlimited access to heaven**. There is unlimited access to heaven for you!

During Jacob's twenty years of serving Laban, Rachel and Leah's father, the Lord tells Jacob to return home to Canaan because God was aware that Laban abused and took advantage of Jacob's willingness to serve (Gen. 31.12). Jacob did not leave Laban's abuse until he received permission from God. Interestingly, God allowed Jacob to remain in Laban's town until God caused Jacob to acquire wealth.

Although he was being taken advantage of, lied to, and abused by Laban, God made certain that Jacob would leave with a wealth of valuables.

If you are in a situation that does not seem like it is going well for you and in your favor, do not leave that situation until God opens the door for you to leave. Do not run away from that situation until you get the permission from God to leave. Some people are so quick to leave one ministry to attend another church, and they are so quick to walk away from situations in where they find themselves being treated unfairly. Meanwhile, God is waiting for them to receive the wealth of wisdom, knowledge, and understanding they will need to take them onto the next temporary rest stop. When Jacob journeyed, he took rest stops, and it was in Beth'el, a rest stop formerly known as Luz, that Jacob had an encounter with God.

The Lord is saying, *"Never get to a place of rest where you leave without receiving everything valuable I have to give you for your onward journey!"* During your journey with God, there will be certain places where God will temporarily have you sow seeds, gain knowledge, experience customs never imagined, and receive blessings while seemingly being drained of our dignity, self-worth, and respect. Jacob never worried because he held onto the promise God made to him that He will not leave Jacob until He is finished giving him everything He had promised him.

When Jacob stopped in Gilead, Laban caught Jacob and they reconciled, but Jacob remained so he could rest for the journey. When he awoke God sent angels to meet him (Gen. 32.1). When the angels met him this time, Jacob renamed Gilead *Mahanaim*. God sent angels to Jacob to reassure him that He was concerned with Jacob. Be open to Divine encounters from God and visitations from the angels He sends.

As Jacob continues to journey, he reaches the Jabbok River and encounters a Man whom he wrestles and struggles with all night. He sees the man's face and renames this place Peniel because this is where he met God face to face. The next time Jacob has a Divine encounter is when he returns to Beth'el where God reveals Himself to Jacob as El'Shaddai. During every encounter before this special encounter, God says he is the God of Abraham and Isaac, but this time He re-introduces Himself as Almighty God, El Shaddai, and changes Jacob's name to Israel. When God reveals Himself to us, we come to know Him on a more intimate level, but He gives us character and we discover our purpose; and there's great purpose in the name Israel!

The encounters you have with God will totally change the landscape of your very being. They will transform your character, your identity, and your life. I've had several life-changing Divine encounters thus far, and I have been changed, but I'm still willing to be transformed even more. Remember, God will not stop until He is finished. As I write this, I received greater insight and greater confidence in His word that says, *"Being confident of this very thing, that He who has begun a good work in you will complete it until the day of Jesus Christ;"* (Philippians 1.6NKJV). The Bible states:

> *"There has never been the slightest doubt in my mind that the God that started this great work in you would keep at it and bring it into a flourishing on the very day Christ Jesus appears."* (Phillippians 1.6 MSG)

You may not be convinced that God's hand is on your life, and you need to hear it from someone God has sent. Therefore, I declare unto you that the Lord is with you and He has not given up you. He is not going to stop until His promises for you have been completed. I say, pick up your faith and take your faith to another level in Christ. God is moving in your spirit even as you read this book. Do not lose hope, stop getting frustrated, and do not become impatient. There is more for you to accomplish here on earth. A wealth of spiritual knowledge and a greater understanding of who Christ is and His wisdom is coming, and greater responsibility is coming with the elevation and promotion from God. God has not forgotten you. Perhaps the moments you have had with God recently have not been as exciting as previous encounters. God has not forgotten you. There are more supernatural manifestations on their way to you. You are not disqualified; you are qualified, and you are on your way to greater things; even better than what it has been. Hallelujah!

CHAPTER VI

The Prayer Agreements

As I conclude this book about prayer there are realities that I must share with you, which I call agreements that you must make with yourself. These agreements will help you to be better informed with what God is doing and what God wants for you.

The first agreement is obedience. Obedience causes God's Word to come alive in your life. If you are not willing to be obedient to God's Word, the prayer you pray will not manifest. **You cannot expect God to move unless you are willing to walk in obedience.** God is not truly concerned with the ritual of prayer as He is more concerned with obedience. Whenever I hear someone talk about King Saul's sacrifice and how God prefers our obedience, I never hear about Saul's ignorance to obedience and sacrifice. What I want you to understand about Saul is that he was so religious that he was doing a religious ritual of making a sacrifice to God. He was offering God a sacrifice from a conditioned mindset that stemmed from what he was taught; and he missed the "why" of making sacrifices. In other words, he knew what he was doing in addition to being disobedient, but did not truly understand why he would make a sacrifice. **Sacrifices that are made to God are necessary, but our obedience to God's instructions is utterly necessary.** Please do not pray with an attitude that communicates, "if I pray in a certain fashion God is more inclined to answer my prayers." Religion teaches people how to pray prayers during a certain season because of the ritualistic importance, and when that particular season is over some people will not pray those prayers again until that same season returns. This was the mindset of Saul. He offered a sacrifice to God with a mindset that translates as, "Sacrifices will make things better." After Samuel learns that Saul was disobedient to the instructions of God, the Message Bible records Samuel's lecture explaining the value of obedience stating:

> *"Do you think all God wants are sacrifices; empty rituals just for show. He wants you to listen to him! Plain listening is the thing, not staging a lavish religious production."*
> (1 Sam. 15.22MSG)

If you want God to move and respond on your behalf then be obedient to what His word says, what the Holy Spirit audibly speaks to you, and to what God's true messenger ministers to you as it is in accordance with God's Word. In order for you to receive what God's messengers say to you, you must know what God's Word says. If you do not know what God's Word states, you will accept anything from anyone that sounds good. Therefore, obey God's Word and you will see great prosperity enter your life.

The second agreement is that you must appear on the battleground to fight. In other words, **after you wage war, engage in the warfare!** The reality is that we do not wrestle against flesh and blood, but we do wrestle against powers, principalities, rulers of darkness of this age, and spiritual wickedness in heavenly places. This means you must be aware that there is an evil force that will attempt to combat various areas of your life. Satan has angels ready to carry out his plans to destroy, tempt, steal, accuse, trick, seduce, and to persuade you that your faith in Christ is useless. Therefore, whenever you pray a prayer for God's will to be performed in your life, the enemy will come to destroy that prayer and suck the life out of that prayer, and you. The enemy attempts to steal the joy you have after making powerful prayer declarations over your life and the world. When you pray, immediate retaliation happens in the spirit realm. When Daniel prayed for revelation to a dream an angel was sent by God to add understanding. (Daniel 10). You may be thinking, "That just happened to Daniel. That can't happen to me because I'm not special and anointed as Daniel was." Please know that with God there is no evaluation and comparison made about who has a greater anointing, a greater power, who is more special, or inherently gifted. God does not operate on terms of strong anointing, but He operates and uses us based on our obedience to Him. God will use you based on if He can trust you as a result of your obedience to Him. Then the Lord will give you a greater anointing to fulfill a great assignment. Daniel's assignment was great so God gave Him greater grace than others to complete the assignment. Satan knew how important Daniel's assignment was that the archangel

Michael had to fight for the messenger sent by God to help Daniel understand the dream. This angel was held by principalities of Persia for twenty-one days before he could actually get to Daniel. (Daniel 10.5-14).

Your prayers are so powerful that the enemy does not like it when you pray, so be aware that when you pray you must show up for battle. Yes, you must be prepared to engage in spiritual warfare. I have prayed prayers waging war against the satanic kingdom, and on a few occasions I failed to appear for battle. Because of my immaturity, I did not realize in those moments that I should have been battling. Therefore, show up to the fight!

The third agreement is to understand that not all prayers will instantly manifest, and we must grow in greater **spiritual maturity**. Our prayers manifest when our faith and spiritual maturity level reaches a certain spiritual age. Sarah may have been old in age when she had her first child, but one of the problems could have been as to why she had yet to give birth was because she was not spiritually mature to handle something that would be birthed in the natural. The challenge is: Are you spiritually mature enough to be responsible for what the Lord gives you to carry, nurture, love, and dedicate back to Him? There is a way to learn how spiritually mature we are and that is by our obedience to God's Word. Spiritual maturity is also revealed in the realm of forgiveness. How quick are you to forgive your enemy? How quick are you to forgive someone who has abused your trust? How quick are you to apologize to someone you may have upset or wronged? How committed are you to quickly getting over grudges and forgiving people? How committed are you to repentance? How serious are you about not committing sin? Jesus teaches us in Mark 11.22-25 that in order for mountains to be moved you must forgive and never doubt. You cannot doubt that your prayers will not be answered.

You may have a huge mountain in your life, which is blocking your vision. Most of the time a spirit of unforgiveness is the mountain that needs to be moved. This mountain is so large that you cannot see past it and you need it to be moved. First, I will tell you that you can move that mountain, but you cannot doubt your ability to move this mountain through prayer. As you begin to move this mountain out of your life, forgive those who have rejected you, embarrassed you, disrespected you, abused you, and taken advantage of your kindness. Forgive them and then God will forgive you and your prayers will not be hindered; but they will be answered.

The fourth agreement is to **pray God's Kingdom and will to be done.** Literally pray that God's Kingdom will be released in your situation as it is in heaven. Say, "God, let thine will be done on earth as it is in heaven." Or, "Let Thine will be done in my marriage as it is in Heaven." Or, "Let Thine will be done in my finances as it is in Heaven." Or, "Let Thine will be done in my life as it is in Heaven." This is my prayer, that the mind of Christ will be glorified in my mind so that I will live in His decrees. **This prayer releases God's supernatural perspective, reality, and solution to resolve the problem occurring in the natural.**

The fifth agreement we must make with ourselves is that fasting must be a big part of our prayer life. Pray for the desire to sacrifice, the willingness to suffer, and to join Christ in His sufferings. To fast and pray is to join Jesus' experience in the wilderness when He fasted for forty days and nights. Fasting is important to the vitality of a believer in Christ because it strengthens the inner man, and the inner man is your spirit.

> *"I pray that God would grant you, according to the riches of His glory to be strengthened with might through His Spirit in the inner man."* (Ephesians 3.16 NKJV)

The riches that are in glory will grant you the strength to pray and fast. Some believers are convinced they do not have to fast and pray, but they are greatly deceived because, *"The flesh wars against the Spirit and the Spirit against the flesh; and they are contrary to one another, so that you do not do the things you wish"* (Gal. 5.17NKJV). During periods of fasting, the stomach begins to dialogue with our thoughts causing us to imagine the melted cheese between two slices of bread along with that bowl of creamy tomato soup. Not only does our flesh become weak when we fast, but other temptations arise, and when they do we must pray so that our spirit becomes stronger. Our spirit can only become strong when it is empowered by the power of the Holy Spirit. He will descend upon your spirit and your flesh will begin to submit to the power that the Holy Spirit has unleashed. The Lord desires that your flesh will walk in agreement with the Spirit of the Living God. How can two walk together, unless they agree? When Jesus' disciples should have been awake and praying, Jesus rebuked them and said, *"The spirit indeed is willing, but the flesh is weak"* (Mark 14.38b). Your spirit is willing to fast, but your flesh is somewhat weak that you sometime give into the cravings you have when you want to be satisfied. God wants you to get to a spiritual place where your spirit will overpower your flesh so that you will walk in the spirit and not the flesh.

The reason why it is important to fast is because temptation is knocking at the door even when you do not realize it. When opportunities come along in the future that may seem good, you must discern if it is God; and not good! **Many things can be good, but not everything is sent by God!**

The sixth agreement is to put life in your faith. Many people pray to God to get great results in their finances and health, yet they doubt. For example, perhaps you have a health condition that you believe will be healed yet somewhere deep inside your thoughts are not connected with your faith. One day you say, "I am healed," and another day you say, "I'm not sure about this." The latter declaration is dead faith while the former declaration is faith full of life. We believe that in Christ there is life and we should live this life in the abundance of God. If your faith is in the Life-Giver then you do not have any reason to allow death-like thoughts, essentially doubtful thoughts, into your faith. The declaration of healing has been decreed.

The centurion knew his servant was healed because there was life in His faith. The centurion did not doubt or second-guess himself or Christ; neither did he question his servant's healing. Something must be said about dead faith because many believers are not full of faith. Most believers believe Christ rose from the dead, but not all believers believe in signs, wonders, and miracles; and they possess little to no faith. Doubt, uncertainty, and second-guessing cannot co-labor with faith. Therefore, put life in your faith.

Lastly, the seventh agreement is that **long-suffering and patience** are fruits of the Spirit that we must allow to flourish in our attitudes. Growth and development occur as a result of deliberate encounters with God. It is true, the Holy Spirit teaches us and shows us things to come. God will show you the gleam of His glory. Prayer can never produce barrenness; there is always insight, hope, joy, and the fullness of Christ when you are intimate with God. There is never a silent moment when it comes to God. He is always speaking, but He is saying that patience and long-suffering must be embraced and embodied. When God is moving, there must be a relentless surrendering for patience and long-suffering that comes from God; and you can do this by having faith in allowing long-suffering and patience to flourish in your character.

There is continuous warfare in the areas that attempt to attack the fruits of long-suffering and patience. Satan's first attack against humanity was the lie about the fruit from the tree of knowledge and good and evil. Your warfare victory is in the area of the fruits of the Spirit. May long-suffering and patience flourish in your attitude; and your prayers will be miraculous prayers that will cause you to prosper!

CHAPTER VII

Prayers that Prosper

This chapter consists of, what I call, prayers that prosper. These prayers are unedited prayers that will move mountains in your life. Do you believe that whatsoever you do will prosper? You cannot forget to daily decree this declaration upon your life! You should no longer question if in fact whatsoever you do will prosper or not, but you must believe in God's word and your approach to everything will change. Prosperity is a huge part of God's plan for your life, which indeed is true: whatsoever you do will prosper! In order for your life to prosper, prayer must be the primary priority of your schedule. Not only must prayer be something you do, but prayer must be who you are! Prayer is what causes your leaves not to whither. Prayer will also cause you to live this life knowing challenges will come, but you can, with a devoted prayer life live in peace as every storm arises. Just because storms arise does not mean you are defeated and just because you feel like nothing is taking place in the natural does not mean a natural manifestation of the supernatural will not happen. God is moving in the supernatural and it is only a matter of time before something miraculous happens. I prophesy to you: it is only a matter of time!

I hope you consider praying these prayers that will cause your life and relationship with Jesus Christ to prosper. I prayed and experienced great breakthrough, deliverance, healing, miracles, signs, and wonders after praying these prayers. Give them a try and see what God does!

Prayer of Giving Everything Over to the Lord

Heavenly Father, I thank You for Your Son Jesus Christ. You loved me so much that You opened your gates to receive me at Your throne regardless of my spiritual, physical, mental, emotional, and financial position. You love me so much that You have given me unlimited access into Your Presence. So God, I pray that You will forgive me of every sin, known and unknown. I want you to know that I am repenting from my sins and I have no plans on turning back to them. God I want to rely on Your Spirit for strength to withstand the wiles of the enemy. I pray that Your word will come alive in my life and that Your word will keep me sober-minded. Your word is a lamp to my feet and a light to my path and I desire to be guided and led by Your Holy Spirit. I desire to be led by Your Spirit and not by my flesh. Whatever I accomplish Lord, I want it to be done by Your power, might, and Spirit, and not by my might, power, and spirit! I have made accomplishments on my own behalf, but I am now at a place where I want you to move mightily through me. Lord, let Your will be done in my life as it is in heaven. In the name of Jesus Christ, I pray, Amen!

Prayer of Repentance

Heavenly Father, I trust and believe that Your Son Jesus Christ has saved me from the penalty of death by dying on the cross and being raised from the dead. And I understand that I am saved and redeemed by the blood of the Lamb, Jesus Christ, and I thank you for what you have done. Even when I was dead in sin, because Your love is great toward me and you are rich in mercy, You made me alive to be united with You. Father, You meant for Your Son, Jesus Christ, and me to sit together in heavenly places so I will rule and reign over sin. So Heavenly Father, I am ready to get rid of, put off, and never turn back to _____ (sin). I desire to be purified from this unrighteousness. Lot's wife turned into a pillar of salt because she did not focus on what was ahead that you had for her to walk into, and God I do not want my life to be stagnant as Lot's wife turned into a pillar of salt. I want to move forward in all that You have planned for me. I believe You have a major Kingdom plan for the life You have given me. I thank you for breathing life into my actions God. I thank You for Your forgiveness and Your power to move me forward with strengthening our togetherness with each other. In the name of Jesus I pray, AMEN!

Spiritual Warfare prayer

Heavenly Father, I come to you in the Name of Jesus and I exalt Your name above all gods, kingdoms, philosophies, and idols. Your wisdom is infinite and Your power is awesome. You have done wonders throughout the earth and this earth belongs to You. Father, not only does this earth belong to You, but _____ (your name, person's name) belong(s) to You! You have commanded me to put on the full armor of God that I may be able to stand in the evil day, and having done all, to stand. I stand with the belt of truth, the breastplate of righteousness, the helmet of salvation, the sword of the Spirit, the shield of faith, and my feet are prepared to speak the truth of the gospel of Jesus Christ. Your name is exalted above all gods, goddesses, demons, spiritual wickedness in heavenly places, principalities, powers, and rulers of darkness of this age. You have called me to bring down strongholds, imaginations, and every high thing that seeks to exalt itself above the knowledge of my Savior Jesus Christ. I bind all the works and strategies of Satan and I lose Your power and truth in my life, in my home, on my job, in my family, in this city, state, region, and nation. I pray against all satanic activity against my health, my family, my job, my finances, my emotions, my relationships, and my spirit. I command all satanic aids, hexes, tentacles, residual effects, spells, tricks, and plans to flee in the name of Jesus once and for all! I pray Psalm 91 over my life, my home, my job, my family, this city, state, region, and nation in the name of Jesus! I am an overcomer and I am more than a conqueror because You are my Lord! The Blood of Jesus be upon everything I am connected. I thank you for victory! In the name of Jesus I pray, AMEN!

Prayer for Finances

Heavenly Father, I thank you for the Son of God, Jesus Christ that has paid every debt in my life. I dedicate my finances to You and I pray for godly wisdom that is taught in Proverbs so that the decisions I make will cause my finances to prosper. You have written in Your word that You have given me the power to create wealth, so please God, let

Your Word that has been spoken and written to come alive in my finances. You said in your word that Your word will not return unto You void, but it will prosper and accomplish the plans and purpose of which the word was sent. I pray for strength and diligence to sacrifice, work, create, sow, and plant financial goodness into my life, my family's life, and those who are in need. I pray against all lethargy and every wavering thought that causes me to quit, fail, and stifle productivity. I dedicate my business, finances, employment, employees, projects, aid, instrument, machinery, contracts, and every future financial blessing and favor to you. I will open my eyes to be more discerning. I ask that you help me to be anxious for nothing, and to pray about everything before I agree! In the name of Jesus Christ, Amen!

Prayer for Wisdom

Heavenly Father, I pray to you in the name of Jesus because I need your wisdom and your Light to direct my paths. Lord I confess my faults and sins in every area area of my life; in my finances, relationships, employment, family, and any other place I may not have knowledge of; bring those areas to my understanding and I pray Jesus that you will show me where I am misguided. God give me your wisdom and send men and women of God that will give me godly counsel about areas in my life where I am uncertain. I pray in the name of Jesus Christ of Nazareth. Amen!

Prayer for Marriage

Heavenly Father, I thank You for making us Your bride. I wait patiently and with joy for the return of Your Son Jesus Christ. I dedicate my marriage to You and I also dedicate my spouse to You Lord. I pray that Your Kingdom will come in my marriage as it is in heaven. I pray that our marriage will honor You and obey Your decrees and commands as it relates to the Biblical foundations and doctrine of marriage according to faithfulness, love, submission toward one another, and Mark 10.6-9. I pray Hebrews 13.4 and I pray Proverbs 19.14 over my spouse and Proverbs 20.6-7 over my spouse. I pray 1 Cor. 13 over our marriage and Ephesians 5.22-33. Let the love we have for You transcend into marriage, but let not our love that we have for each other become idolatrous. Let Galatians 5.22&23 abound in our marriage. I pray that you would bring us to a place of agreement in prayer. Have us not to live in the mindset of Ananias and Sapphira, but cause us to stand in/for truth. Bless our intimacy and let it prosper; bless our finances and let it prosper; bless our businesses, passions, gifts, talents, and employment and let them prosper; and bless our children and let them prosper. Let us be a blessing to other marriages. I pray that this prayer will cause heaven to open on our marriage based on 2 Chronicles 7.14 and John 14.13&14. I thank You Father for what will occur because of this prayer in Your name Jesus, Amen!

Prayer for Children

Heavenly Father, I pray in the name of Jesus for my children, grandchildren, god children, and spiritual sons and daughters and I commit them over to you. I welcome them with Your love as You taught us in Mark 9.37. I pray against every vice, peer, influence, problem, discouragement, misunderstanding, false teaching of deception and lie that causes them to stumble based on Matthew 18.6, and I trust in your word that assures me that You are the Vindicator. As You Lord have vindicated me, vindicate the children based on Psalm 138.8! I pray that you protect them from abandonment, pedophilia, all divers of abuse, kidnapping, child sacrifice, rape, peer pressure to use drugs and to participate in sexual activity, learning disabilities, obesity, poverty, low self-esteem, spells, hexes, demonic activities and games, and early childhood catastrophic crisis. Bless them with the wisdom, knowledge, and understanding of your Son, Our Lord Jesus Christ. Set their hearts on fire for You and baptize them with Your Holy Spirit. Teach them to live in Your purpose and for them to walk worthy of their calling. Let Your will be done in their lives and it is in Jesus' name I pray, Amen!

Prayer for Unity with God

Heavenly Father, I pray to You in the name of Jesus! I pray that as Your Son, Jesus Christ, was unified and one with You, that I will be co-joined to Your mission for my life. I pray against anything that wants our relationship to fail and engage in the warfare against Satan who is attempting to contend for my life with Your Son Jesus Christ. I pray that as Jesus spoke what He heard You say, and what He saw You do, I pray that I speak Your words that are Spirit and Life. I pray that I do the works of healing, forgiving, delivering, and restoring in the name of Jesus! God if we are one, people will know that You are God and God alone. They will know that there is nobody like You. In the name of Jesus, Amen!

Daily Prophetic Declaration

I declare, in the name of Jesus, that my leaves will not whither, but whatsoever I do will prosper. My finances are blessed because I live by God's wisdom! I live and stand under an open heaven where the blessings of God are pouring out and drenching my life. My relationships are blessed because I am unified with God! I call forth order in my life! I decree synergy and synchronization with God! I am free from every sickness and disease that once caused me to lose sleep due to worry. I call forth peace in my house, peace on my job, peace in my family, and peace in my mind! I decree I am saved and redeemed by the blood of the Redemptive Lamb of God! In the name of Jesus, Amen!

About the Author

Having experienced many difficult life changing experiences, Donald Williams, learned that prayer is the "payment bond" that insures and assures healing, deliverance, forgiveness, prosperity, reconciliation, and miracles. Donald Williams served as the pastor of Prayer at his home church just before becoming the founding pastor of the Miracle Center International Ministries in Columbia, MD. He has organized prayer shut-ins, harp and bowl prayer and prophetic ministry, and has prayed for those that were once bound that now live in freedom. He has experienced people announced dead by medical doctors and through prayer these individuals live today. He has also prayed for people that have received life threatening and death dealing prognosis and diagnosis, and through prayer, these individuals are disease free and still living to this day. Pastor Donnie is a witness to miraculous transformations such as troubled minds being restored to peace, disease and sickness being miraculously transformed through divine healing, and oppression and possession being miraculously transformed to liberation and freedom. It is only by prayer that nations dealing with nationwide sicknesses and economic disaster are brought to healing and prosperity. Since prayer will work for a nation, it will work for you. Pray and watch everything you do to prosper. PRAY!